TRANSFORM
HOW YOU PERFORM
IN TENNIS

Mental skill development
for competitive confidence

Helen K. Emms

lıp

First published in 2012 by:

Live It Publishing
27 Old Gloucester Road
London, United Kingdom.
WC1N 3AX
www.liveitpublishing.com

ISBN 978-1-906954-17-8 (hbk)

Contents

My Tennis Development

 Personal Data

Name:

Age:

My current rating/ranking is:

My favourite sports star:

The 3 personal qualities they have that I want are:

What I want to get from completing this program:

Foreword

I have had the pleasure of working with Helen and being coached by her over the last 5 years. Whilst I specialize in the physical strength and conditioning aspects of developing peak performing athletes, specifically preparing them to achieve International standards in their sport, the inclusion of the mental skills within my work has made a significant difference to the speed of improvement in players and their overall achievements. Without doubt, mental skill development needs to take place as early as possible, alongside the technical and physical development and it is we technical and physical coaches who are key to this happening. The way in which we coach our clients has a major impact on their mental skill development, whether we realize it or not. This book is as helpful for the coach as it is for the player.

Having worked with Tennis Coaches and International tennis players at one of the top Tennis Academies in the UK, Helen's work helping players and coaches to integrate mental skill development into their training was considered one of the most significant coaching contributions to their award of International High Performance Centre status by the NTC.

This book reveals the underlying principles to developing Mental Toughness by developing the necessary mental skills during training that are essential for Performance. These skills need to be practiced and cannot be just turned on when a player steps onto the court.

Helen guides players, positively, through the process of goal setting and recording from a mental skill perspective. This means that you are asked to reflect more on your level of focus and motivation than whether you hit your forehand where you wanted to. You are asked questions such as how do you know you were successful and what has helped you to feel more confident? All the time, you are guided to give your attention to the process of tennis rather than getting mentally caught up in results and outcomes. Of course the process always leads to the outcomes, but the mind needs to be trained to let go of the outcomes so as to direct attention into the present moment.

As a general principle, if your mind is not in the right place, your performance will always be sub-optimal. Working on yourself to ensure your mind and emotional state are optimal is crucial to your success. This book supports you to achieve exactly that. It gets you to re-prioritise your thinking about your tennis development and rightly so, because the mind-set of any player will determine their overall success in the game, given their physical and technical talent. Enjoy your journey of self-discovery and the results it is sure to bring when you follow this programme with a positive mental intention.

Daz Drake
Strength & Conditioning Expert
Director of the Youth Coach Network (YCN)

Introduction

The fact that you have invested in this short program of development to transform how you perform means that you are interested in getting better results out of your tennis quickly, both in training and in competitions. You may be someone who trains really well but never takes that level of performance to the competitive arena, constantly feeling as if you are underperforming. You may be someone who aspires

Confidence is the most important mental skill that you must develop to transform your performance

to be an international tennis player and needs some guidance from a Peak Performance Specialist to get your best results more often. Or, you may be someone who wants to have more fun and enjoy competitive success no matter what level of tournament you play. Whatever your reason for investing in this program the single key to success and therefore the most important mental skill you can develop, that will transform your performance, is your confidence.

Confident players will always achieve more success than the rest and that doesn't happen by accident or luck and contrary to popular belief it doesn't always happen as a function of winning. Building confidence is actually a mental skill that has to be actively developed. It is about being mindful, which means that you do everything for a purpose. It isn't something that is there when you are doing well and gone when you are doing badly, although this will be most people's experience of their confidence.

Through the series of activities that you will undertake in this 2 part program you will learn to develop deep enduring confidence that holds up under pressure. Some people think that winning is the thing that makes you confident, but confidence is not just about your results; it's about much more than that. Confident performers know how to get the best out of themselves under pressure, they find solutions not problems, they have beliefs that support them, strategies they follow when things aren't going their way and they have great control over their emotional state and thought processes. In essence, confident performers get the best out of themselves even when they are not winning, which means they feel good more often.

You may not have realized before now that how you measure your success will either support or damage your confidence, which means that learning to measure your success effectively is going to help to transform how you perform. Therefore, throughout this program, one of the ways you will be developing your confidence is through effective monitoring and evaluation. The more effort you put into this process the more you will benefit from it. If you cheat you will gain nothing. If you work hard at it your confidence will soar and you will transform how you perform.

The mental discipline required for effective monitoring and evaluation is critical to your tennis development for the following reasons:

1. You need to be aware of where you are now – let's call this A
2. You need to be aware of where you want to go – let's call this B
3. You need to be aware of what you need to do to get from A to B
4. You need to be aware of whether you are "on track" to get to B

If you are aware of these things you will be able to manage your development knowing that you are moving in the direction you want – to achieve your goals. And if you find that you are not moving in the right direction you can take swift action to bring yourself back on track at the earliest opportunity. Just imagine yourself as the pilot of an aircraft. The pilot constantly has to readjust the direction the aircraft is taking, so that they end up at their destination. The same is true for you. You are the pilot of your own aircraft.

This program is in 2 parts. The first part gives you a great deal of background information that you need to be aware of to be able to perform at your best more often. There are a series of tasks associated with each aspect of this part of the program that you should complete as you go. The second part is a log-book that lasts for 3 months. Some of the information you come up with in the first part can be used in your completion of the log-book. Please do not be deceived by how short this program is. There is a great deal of work for you to do to complete this program effectively. You are likely to revisit the text in Part 1 of the program on several occasions and I would recommend that you extend Part 2 indefinitely beyond your completion of the initial 12 weeks.

As a function of what you learn from Part 1 of this program and as you complete the log-book in Part 2 you will be developing some of the other key mental skills that are necessary for you to transform how you perform: such as, discipline, emotional control and concentration. You will also learn to develop other key skills for performing, such as a developing a quiet non-critical mind, being present

If you commit to doing the exercises you will transform how you perform. If you just read, nothing will change

and effective monitoring and evaluation. All of these skills are necessary for you to free yourself up to perform at your highest level.

In summary, this program teaches you how to be successful at goal setting and goal management so that you can manage this process yourself. It also helps you develop the key mental skills that are required for you to perform well, such as effective problem solving, confidence building, concentration, effective beliefs, the process of learning and change and the difference between the training and performance mind-sets. As you complete the exercises in the program you will find that you have a better understanding of your game, feel more confident about what you do that works and improve your focus and discipline. You will become more mindful, which means you will do things for a purpose that supports your desired aim... to transform how you perform. As a result of this, you will have the awareness to change your game and progress at a faster rate. This is a program of 'doing' and not just 'reading'. If you just read, nothing will change. If, on the other hand, you make a mental commitment to yourself to work hard at developing these key skills and you commit to doing the exercises, I guarantee you will transform how you perform.

What Is Your Performance About?

Before thinking about what goals are right for your performance, you first need to be aware of what your performance is about? Yes, it is about winning or performing your best, but the question that you must answer is: "What do you need to do to achieve these outcomes that you want?" The answer to this question, irrespective of your playing standard, is to deliver your tactical plan on the court against your opponent to the best of your ability on the day – we can call this your 'strategy'.

If you are a professional, part of your performance will be about entertaining others. After all you are being paid to do a job and that job is to provide a great sporting spectacle for those watching. It sometimes helps amateur players to think this way, even if there isn't anyone watching. Using your imagination to think that you are performing for the pleasure of others can help you to control your emotional state and behavior. After all, if you really were playing center court at Wimbledon would you throw your racket over the fence? Maybe, but hopefully, when you imagine yourself as someone who is entertaining others it can help you to control yourself.

Your performance is also about you testing your technical, physical and mental skill development. The performance is effectively the testing ground, to see how your skills hold up under pressure. If they don't, this is telling you that you have not developed your skills to the level that they need to be and you can take what you learn about yourself back onto the training ground. Sometimes players think that they should perform well because they train well, but this is not the case. This way of mentally approaching competing, with expectations, will cause you to feel more pressure than it will help you to perform well. Instead, the competitive arena should be the place to feel relaxed and have fun. The training ground is really the place that you should put yourself under pressure to perform and push your limits. In my experience of working with many amateur elite tennis players there is a tendency to operate the other way around: training doesn't push them hard enough and they feel too much pressure when performing. This is a bad combination and the result is always under-performance.

Make sure your goal setting includes all aspects of your performance

One way I encourage players to think about their performance is in terms of ingredients, just like baking a cake. If I want to bake a cake I will get a recipe which tells me the ingredients I need and their exact quantities. I will mix those ingredients together as instructed and then bake the cake in the oven at the right temperature for the stated time. If I decide to put in different ingredients or not follow the recipe then I will certainly get a different cake. Maybe it will be a success and maybe it won't. The problem comes when I don't know what I have put into my cake because this makes it difficult for me to know what works and what doesn't, or how I did well and how to improve it.

Tennis is just like baking a cake. There are some basic ingredients that you need to put in to get the outcomes you want. You need to know what to put in to get the result you want and also to identify when you are putting in different ingredients so that you can know you are baking a different cake. Then you can work out what is successful and what isn't. In changing the ingredients of your tennis cake, however, I would recommend that you adopt a scientific approach and change one thing at a time so that you can see the effect of this change. All too often players change too many things and it becomes impossible to know what ingredients have created what impact. The contribution of your mental skill ingredients will have a significant effect on the quality of the cake you bake. Simple thoughts or a slight shift in your emotional state can change your cake from a flop to a world beater!

All aspects of your development (mental/emotional, physical/ physiological, tactical and technical) have the capacity to limit or enhance your success as a performer. Therefore, it is important that you develop all these aspects to give you the best chance of playing at your highest potential. When we increase our capability or competence at what we do we feel more confident. So in developing your mental skills and controlling your emotional and physiological responses you are going to increase your competence at dealing with things across the whole of your life as well as in tennis. As a result you will feel more confident in yourself and raise your sense of self-esteem.

Task...

Now, take some time to identify the key ingredients for your game and write them in the box below. Be very clear about these ingredients so that if someone else were to read your ingredients they would know exactly what you mean. For example, if you write breathing as one of your ingredients I really don't know what that means as there are different types of breathing – breathing that gets you fired up and breathing that calms you down. So be clear in your description as this will help you to commit to your own development of these skills.

Mental ingredients	Physical ingredients	Tactical ingredients	Technical ingredients
E.g. Deep belly breathing, slowly in and out to control nerves & over excitement			

Goal Setting
For Success

All great performers set goals for themselves. They will set what are called 'outcome goals', which are goals such as winning events, increasing their ranking/positioning and earning money (at the professional level) and they will set what are called 'process goals', which are based around their performance such as improving their backhand slice, increasing the speed of their 1st serve, improving their response to errors, improving tactical decision making, etc. The process goals that most players set have a technical bias, often without consideration

Make sure your goal setting includes all aspects of your performance

for the mental, emotional and physiological factors that influence their technical delivery. Setting process goals to develop these other important factors, is necessary to support your technical and tactical development. The goals that you set from now on should be carefully considered and include the development of your mental skills (such as effective thinking and processing), emotional factors (such as dealing with frustration, excitement and nerves) and physiological factors (such as coping with tension and choking). There are some easy rules to follow, that we will explore later, to make sure that you are working on the right things for your game.

The reasons why it is important for you to set process goals and manage the achievement of those goals are:

- Process goals provide you with the motivation to take action
- They give you energy and something to be determined about achieving
- They provide you with a sense of direction, so you know where you are going
- They provide you with an objective measure of your achievement so that you can plan your next steps
- They are the signposts on the journey to your dream goal
- They are the things you can control, whereas the outcomes you cannot control because others play a part in those outcomes. You can only influence your outcome goals through the achievement of your process goals \

Examples of outcome goals would be:

- The number of events at a specific grade that you want to enter
- The positions within events that you would like to achieve (such as quarter finals, semi finals, finals, winning)
- The number of ITF points you want to get
- The ranking or rating changes that you want to achieve

You will notice that with all these outcome goals you are not 100% in control of whether you get the outcome. Other people can have an impact on your achievements, which is why these goals become something to strive to achieve, but not something you should measure your success by on their own. Below are some examples of performance or process goals. Process goals are far more important for you to measure your success by because you have control over the ingredients you put into them.

- The level of arousal you feel (this is your feeling of being up for it) based on a rating of 1-10 where 5 or 6 is the ideal arousal level
- The % of negative thoughts you have following a mistake and the % of corrective thoughts you have following a mistake
- The number of points you turn around when in a defensive situation (demonstrating a mental attitude of persistence and never giving up)
- Your service effectiveness percentage (effectiveness as an outcome is based on your impact on the opponent), your measure of success though is based on 100% mental commitment to the serve (which means there is no doubt in your mind)
- The percentage of time you do your pre-shot routines
- The percentage of time you problem solve when things aren't going to your tactical plan (rather than getting frustrated)

Task...

Come up with some outcome goals and performance goals in each of the boxes below that you are working towards achieving. Be very clear about these goals and put a timescale next to them, which is by when you will have achieved them.

Outcome Goals	Date by when they will be achieved
Example of an outcome goal: To win 4 grade 4 events and reduce my rating from 8.1 to 7.1	By 30 September 2012

Now decide on the process goals that you will need to achieve to support your attainment of the outcome goals you have listed above.

Performance / Process Goals	Date by when they will be achieved
Example of a mental process goal: *75% effective routines (measure of effective - is a full & engaged focus achieved before the point starts)*	*By 30 August 2012*

We will focus on the development of your mental skills for performance next.

Reminder... your performance is about:

1. Your tactical impact on your opponent
2. Entertaining others
3. Testing all aspects of your skill development
4. The effectiveness of the ingredients you put in

Mental Skill Development For Performance

You may be new to the idea of mental skill development and wondering why the mental skills are so important. You may have already read a bit about mental skills or even received coaching before now. You may be like most people and know that mental skills are important but not yet had the chance to do much about your own mental skill development. Whatever your start point is, it doesn't matter. What is important though is that you have a good understanding of why the mental skills are so important and what sort of mental skills we are talking about.

Here is an exercise to help you to experience the power of your mind body connection. Imagine now that you are cutting into a nice, fresh, big juicy zesty lemon. You can feel the waxy surface of the lemon on your finger-tips. As you imagine cutting through the lemon with the sharp knife you can hear it slicing through the skin. Smell the zest tingling your nose, and as it does so splashes of lemon shoot up and one catches your mouth. You can almost feel the sharpness of the knife as it penetrates the lemon and the juices are running freely onto the surface. Imagine now picking up a slice of that lemon, feel the cool juice running across your fingers as you put it into your mouth, and you will notice that your body has responded and your mouth will be salivating.

> *Your mind and body are intimately and intricately connected. One affects the other*

If you didn't get a salivation response, it either means that you have never come across a lemon before and therefore don't have a clue about lemons, or, the most likely scenario is that you are reading the words but not engaging in the process of sensory imagery. There are 2 things to consider here. Firstly, you can always choose to fully engage in what you are doing, or not. Your level of engagement will have a massive impact on your ability to create significant changes in your performance. Secondly, sensory imagery is a vital skill to master to become an effective performer. All our experiences in life are multi-sensory because they involve all our 5 senses; sight, sound, touch, smell and taste. Our experiences will involve some of our senses more than others. So, for example when you are playing tennis you will engage your visual and touch sense and maybe your hearing too. You are unlikely to engage your taste that much. We learn to respond to the events we experience in a specific way and when we do, this response becomes linked with the specific event. This linking process is called anchoring – which really means that our sensory experience has been linked with a physiological or emotional response. Imagine

if you played tennis and didn't give any attention to ho‸
on your racket. If you did this you would never be c‸
ball control, because you would have no sense of the imp‸
physical connection with the ball. Learning to use multi-sensε‿
imagery is an excellent skill to have as a Performer.

The anchoring process that I have just mentioned is also the reason that you respond the way you do when things don't go your way. Your frustration when the ball doesn't do what you expect is an anchored response. So, you will also need to learn to un-anchor specific responses to enable you to maintain the peak performance state that we will talk about later. You are likely to need specialist help with this process because it isn't always that simple to achieve.

Reminder...

You can always choose to fully engage in what you are doing, or not, and your level of engagement will have a massive impact on your ability to create significant changes in your performance

So, going back to our lemon tasting exercise, the reason you had a salivation response is because your mind and body are intricately and intimately connected. This very simply means that what goes on in your mind has an impact on your body and vice versa. In fact, science shows that your mind is also stored in your body, so you should be thinking in terms of your 'mind-body' as being one thing. You can work on your body to help your mind, as when you get much fitter and stronger physically you can feel more confident in your ability to outlast your opponents. And you can work on your mind to help your body, as when you focus on your deep breathing you can learn to control your nerves and anxiety, or you can over-ride tiredness through mental strength.

Your mind is the controller of your interpretation of your experiences. This means your mind controls your thoughts, feelings, memories, the way in which you process information, the way you measure success, your interpretation of events, your desires and fears. All these factors will contribute to your success, or lack of it. It is a fact that your mental skills have a direct impact on your emotional and physiological responses and it is a fact that you can develop all the effective mental skills that you need to achieve the highest levels of success. You have to learn to use the power of your mind effectively, which as I mentioned earlier, can mean de-linking some of your anchored responses to situations that happen.

Developing your mental skills by taking control of your mind will therefore help you to control your emotions and your physiology and when you have this level of control over yourself, you also think more effectively.

Your character is not fixed, it is something you develop over your life-time through your interpretation of your experiences

The reality is that there are ways to think, feel, behave, process and evaluate that lead to success and there are also less effective and efficient ways of doing these things. The challenge you have is that you have developed habits and those habits become your normal way of 'being', whether they are effective or not. Contrary to popular belief, your mental functioning, character and psyche are not fixed, they are developed over time based on your interpretation of your experiences. This means it is always possible to learn to be more effective. So in developing your mental skills you are going through the process of changing your bad habits and replacing them with more effective habits. When you learn to use your mind (including emotional and physiological responses) effectively you can transform how you perform, easily and effortlessly.

Developing your mental skills is the same, and just as important, as developing the other aspects of your game. It requires you first to know what you need to do, then to practice the skills (with feedback) and eventually transition the skill into a habit. Habits take time and effort to develop, just like developing a great serve or forehand, which is why this program is designed for a minimum of 12 weeks. The people who fail to develop their mental skills effectively are those who expect things to happen very quickly and without a great deal of effort. They give up too easily. Or they think that their mental skills are fixed and cannot be changed, which we know is not true.

One thing to bear in mind is that you are already using your mental skills. How you currently perform mentally will already be strongly influencing the results you get. If you are getting great results when performing under pressure then you can be assured that what you are doing is working well for you. If on the other hand you are not getting the results you feel you should under performance pressure, then you will want to pay more attention to developing your mental skills to get the best out of your abilities. Putting the same mental ingredients in will help you to get the same result (under the conditions you are performing). So, you just need to make sure you get the result you want and if not, change the ingredients. However, if you perform at a higher level or you find your performance deteriorates even though you are still training your technical and physical skills

> *"Whether you think you can change or not, you will always be right"*
> Henry Ford

effectively, then again you will need to work on your mental skills to learn to operate at a higher level of mental performance. The mental skills that work at 7/8 years old are not going to work at 14/15 and certainly not at a professional level. In the same way that you need to continually improve your technical competences, so you need to improve your mental competences.

The mental skills you develop are fluid and are only limited by your resistance to changing them. In other words, your mental development has no limitations, other than those you impose through your beliefs and thoughts. As a general principle; if you think things about your mind are fixed you will make no effort to change them, so if you see your character or way of being (mentally) as something that is fixed it will remain that way. If instead you see that you can change these things you will give yourself the chance to change because you will put the effort in to change!

Have you ever considered what specifically we mean when we refer to 'mental skills'? Most people think of 'mental robustness', being 'mentally tough' and other such phrases, but what are we really talking about? How do we achieve mental toughness? Below are some things that I consider to be mental skills and these should become part of your development as a performer:

- Effective Thinking
- Learning
- Awareness
- Concentration/Focus
- Emotional Responses
- Communication Skills
- Problem Solving
- Decision Making
- Handling Uncertainty
- Effective Planning
- Developing Identity
- Embracing Change
- Expectation Management
- Error Management
- Perception
- Choice / Consequences
- Meditation
- Arousal Management
- Independence
- Trust

- Mental Silence
- Self-Discipline
- Mental Processing
- Managing Distractions
- Mental Commitment
- Confidence Building
- Coping Strategies
- Empowering Beliefs
- Handling Conflict
- Monitoring & Evaluation
- Motivation & Desire
- Routines & Habits
- Tactical Thinking
- Strategies for Success
- Measurement of Success
- Effective Breathing
- Peak State Control
- Stress Management
- Personal Responsibility
- Engagement (Presence)

These are just some of the mental skills you could develop, and I am hoping that having listed them here you can look through and identify the ones that will have the biggest impact for you in your performance. We won't be covering them all here because each one is a program on its own, but if you would like further information on any specific topic above, or more information on developing yourself as a Peak Performer, or if you would like to qualify to coach others to become a Peak Performer, please contact me at **www.academyforpeakperformance.co.uk** ⟶

Now, let's direct our attention to the key skills for performing that will also have a positive impact on the development of your confidence. These skills are developing the performance mind-set, learning effective measurement and evaluation, learning about the causes of errors and how to problem solving, increasing intensity in training, how to manage the learning cycle and change and building confidence through positive labeling. Firstly, complete the exercise below and we will then move onto defining the performance mind-set.

Task...

When you look through the list above, which are the key mental skills that you would like to develop (pick the ones you think would have the biggest impact on your game now)? List them in the box below and then identify one action you are going to take to develop that skill further.

Mental skills to develop	Action I can take now
Example: Emotional responses	*Example: I am going to use my routines and deep breathing to stay calm between points and stay focused on my tactical plan*

Defining The Performance Mind-Set

There are some key differences between the mind-set for training and the mind-set for performing. You need to develop the effective mental skills for performing in order to release yourself, to play without fear. Here are some examples of the differences:

Training Mind-Set

1 Active mind with technical thinking

2 Continuous evaluation during the session

3 Emphasis on development and getting it perfect

4 Trying hard to get the skill right, going over the same skill, breaking it down to drill it

5 Processing what is wrong and correcting it through repetition

6 No need to trust yourself to get it right first time because you can have as many goes as you like when training

Performance Mind-Set

1 Quiet mind – no technical thinking

2 No evaluation until after the performance

3 Emphasis on getting the tactical outcome you want, not being perfect

4 Not trying too hard, allowing and going with the flow

5 Recovery from errors (again not seeking perfection)

6 Processing through tactical appreciation, maintaining state and physiology

7 Trust yourself and the process even when things aren't going as you want them to

If you want to be successful within the competitive arena and take the things you are learning into your matches quickly and effectively, then, within your training program you need to spend time developing your 'performance mind-set'.

It is very difficult to just move into the performance mind-set for a competition if you have been practicing with a training mind-set. You can see from the above that they are virtually the opposite of each other. The reason it is difficult if not impossible to just switch from one mind-set to the other is that the training mind-set has become a habit and habits are hard to change. As with all skills, practice takes time and effort. If you haven't

Train your performance mind-set to make it a great habit

trained your performance mind-set you will be unlikely to find it easy to trust yourself to perform when you need to. In the heat of battle, when you start to doubt yourself, you are more likely to do what you have done before (even if it doesn't work) rather than do something you have never done before (even if it might work). This is how habits keep you stuck doing what you have always done. It is also why you might feel that mental skills and character are fixed. They aren't, they are just very strong habits!

Two of the key mental skills that will help you to change are self-awareness and self-discipline. If you become aware that you are doing the same thing (which is ineffective), you can change it. If you remain unaware, you cannot change it and your progress will be slow, if at all. Once you have raised your awareness to how you do what you do, then you need to have the discipline to make the change work. And remember, discipline is a choice and strongly associated with highly successful performers.

Developing The Performance Mind-Set

The quiet mind

Achieving a quiet mind is clearly easier said than done. Try sitting still in a quiet room for a few minutes and relax. See how many thoughts you have come into your mind in a very short space of time. To get to the level of a quiet mind could take years of practice. But practice is essential for you to master this skill. I will always recommend that players get into the practice of meditation. This is not some wacky Eastern thing. It is a very serious practice that will train your mind to stay quiet. Start by practicing

Focus on your breathing to make it work for you

meditation for just a couple of minutes every day either in the evening before you sleep or first thing in the morning as you wake. Sit with your back in an upright position, close your eyes and focus on your breathing. Every time your focus wanders bring it back to your breathing. If you have thoughts that come into your mind imagine putting them on a cloud and get them to float away and then get your attention back to focusing on your breathing. For every breath, focus

27

on it to the exclusion of everything else. Put every thought on a cloud and let it float away. Do not allow your attention to fix on any thought as this will become a distraction.

The part of your mind that you are training will want you to be distracted, so you will have to work hard and be disciplined about letting your thoughts go and staying focused on your breathing. Once you achieve this for a couple of minutes, move up to 5 minutes and then to 10. See if you can get yourself to 20 minutes of meditation a day. You may find some days easier than others. This in itself is interesting and you may find it easier to meditate at a particular time of day, such as the morning or evening. You may find your mind telling you that this is boring, which is simply another distraction. You must master the art of a quiet mind and there really is only one way to achieve that and that is through meditation.

Tactical focus and problem solving

You need to learn to evaluate what you are doing from a tactical perspective rather than from a technical perspective. If you make a mistake the key to you staying in the present moment is to let the mistake go. Over analysis when you make a mistake will cause you to under-perform. Instead, learn to relax the parts of your body that feel tense when you make mistakes and keep

Tell yourself what impact you want to have on your opponent & keep it in your mind

focused on what you want to achieve (tactically). Telling yourself that you want to hit the ball deeper may not be effective. Trying to hit the same shot over and over again in a match, to get it right and prove to yourself that you can do it will also destroy your performance. Instead, tell yourself what impact you want to have on your opponent: for example, get them 2 meters behind the baseline in a defensive position. Keep your mind in the game and not on your technique. Use technical cue words to keep your technique on track and also be aware that you physical and mental state will also impact the delivery of your technique. The more specific and tactically detailed you are with your focus the easier it is for you to achieve what you want. If you are vague or you don't think of anything, or you are critical, you will encourage yourself to play with fear and this will affect your physiology and then your physical movement and technical delivery.

No critical evaluation

One of the biggest distractions is critical evaluation. Notice I have said critical. This means words such as 'rubbish, awful, crap, excellent, fantastic, awesome'. Critical and judgmental evaluations are where we use words that have some feeling attached to them. Even positive evaluations can work against you because as soon as you do something that is not as good, you will be critical of yourself as you compare it to

Be your own best coach. Stop being critical of yourself and stay focused on what you want to achieve

what you did very well before. So the best thing to do is to stop evaluating from this judgmental perspective. You will see that the ball went long or in the net and from this position you can rectify the situation, by focusing on creating the shape of shot that you want (which will go over the net and into the court). This type of evaluation is objective rather than emotional and will help you to remain emotionally in control even when making mistakes. In correcting your errors and maintaining your excellent shots always keep your mind on the shape of the shot you hit and the impact it had on your opponent rather than just saying 'that was awesome'. After the performance you can be more critical of yourself if you wish, but I would recommend that you keep your post match evaluation as objective as possible to avoid linking negative responses to your performances.

Not trying to be perfect

In training the appropriate mind-set most of the time is to become as technically, physically, tactically and mentally competent as you can. Most players will spend a lot of time trying to be technically perfect. They do this through repetition and breaking skills down into small parts to practice at the level of small details. This is entirely appropriate to learn to develop the skills you need to be able to perform at your best. But, this often leads to players developing the mind-set that says mistakes are a problem. It also leads players to become dissatisfied with something that is less than perfect. Most players will have come across Brad Gilbert's book 'Winning Ugly' and whether you like

Effective practice is your goal, not perfection

the book or not, the title is very apt. When you are performing it doesn't matter what it looks like or feels like, it is about getting the job done – getting the win! Anything that gets in the way of that, such as judging your shots as not being good enough, trying to hit the perfect shot when performing and over analysis are a distraction and will result in you under-performing more often. You have to learn that perfection is not your goal: practice is your goal! Practicing to perform is essential and practicing the qualities of a performance mind-set is your goal. If you work on developing the performance mind-set in your training you will give yourself the best chance of success in your performances.

Not trying too hard

Too often, and especially when things aren't going well, players start to try too hard to make up for what is going wrong and can easily become physically tight, mentally tense and start to force shots, as if trying to make something happen. This is a natural tendency and yet it can be the opposite of what is actually required. When you try too hard your muscles naturally tense up and you force things rather than using your natural rhythmical power. Trying too hard results in your perception (of the ball) slowing down, your movement slowing down and a loss of ball control. Sometimes players will slap shots, having partially given up. They can get a couple of flashy winners which may result in them settling down again, relaxing a bit and they may even start playing well. But this is a risky strategy and all too often performance will deteriorate overall. Learning to focus on the right things when your game isn't going as you want must be part of your training. For this you need to be clear about what your 'recovery strategies' are. The easiest recovery strategy is to get your focus back to your plan. If your problems are because your plan is not working you first need to check whether it is your execution that is ineffective

The Law of Reversed Effect states that the harder you try the more difficult things become

rather than the plan? If it is your execution then you need to make sure your emotional and physiological state is good, your thoughts are supporting you and that you are moving well. Correcting these things will help you to be more effective delivering your plan. If it is the wrong plan then you need to be clear about how you adapt your plan to have the effect that you want. Specifically, you need to learn to regain your rhythm by relaxing your focus,

Recovery strategies help you to control mental stress & physical tension when things aren't going well

moving your feet and releasing your shots. You also need to learn to stay focused on delivering your tactical plan without expecting to be perfect. And you need to trust that what you are doing will give you your best results. Sometimes we deceive ourselves into thinking that if we try harder at least we can say we tried. Instead of just trying harder and muscling the ball, I want you to think of being smarter, which means staying relaxed, moving your feet, maintaining a strong determination to get behind the ball and mentally staying focused on the right things.

Learning to trust

Trust takes an act of faith, and faith really can move mountains. Learning to trust yourself, though, may be one of the hardest things you have to learn to do. After all, how can you learn to trust something that isn't working as you want it to? Many players who struggle with trusting themselves are also those who are only happy if they are achieving their expectations or perfection. So in this case, they will only trust if they get the outcome they want. Of course it would be great to be able to get the outcome you want all of the time, but this is not the way that tennis or the world works. It is unrealistic to expect this because there are no guarantees of outcomes and there are no guarantees that you will hit the ball the way you want to or at the level that you are capable of. The only thing

Trust takes an act of faith... and faith moves mountains

you can guarantee is to give your best effort to putting in the right ingredients to give you the best chance of success. You have full control over what you do but you don't have full control over your results.

You need to learn to trust in your abilities (rather than criticize yourself for being less than perfect). Trust that no matter how you perform on any day, if you continue to train effectively, you will become more competent and successful. You need to trust in yourself and what you can put into your performances and accept that you don't always have control over what you get out. In other words, you need to learn to trust unconditionally and you need to learn the art of patience. If you focus more on what you are putting into your game and less on what you get out of it you will more easily see your improvements, which will further reinforce your trust in yourself. If you only put effort in on the basis of getting something out in that moment, your career in tennis could be very short lived. As you become a great problem solver in tennis you will also learn to trust that no matter what happens you can cope. This is an invaluable skill that will support you beyond your tennis career. Learning to trust that all the hours you are putting in will amount to something, even if you can't see it right now is a hugely valuable skill for your life as well as your tennis. It may help to think of yourself as a bank account. You are putting lots of small deposits into your account and you have to accrue a big sum before the interest you earn becomes noticeable. Don't expect a big payout of interest on one small deposit because you won't get it.

Developing the performance mind-set takes a lot of practice, just like any skill that you need to learn, and you must build this time into your training. An ideal time to do this is when playing point play situations and practice matches. If you normally go into point play situations and practice matches with your mind on winning or practicing the technique that you are working on then you are missing a great opportunity to develop your performance skills. Too many players see these training matches as something serious and put all their efforts into trying to beat their opponent, often reverting to their old habits, rather than seeing these times as an opportunity to develop their performance skills. This is a big error in thinking and will result in a slower transition of skills to the performance court. Learning to be less critical of yourself when training is also going to support your performances. Instead of being critical, learn to become an excellent problem solver on the court. Then nothing will catch you out or cause you to feel stressed. Problem solving is a key mental skill and one that really has a massive impact on your confidence. There is no better feeling than the confidence that comes when you know that no matter what happens out there, you can cope with it.

Task...

Which aspect of the performance mind-set are you going to work on now? In the box below list some of the actions you are going to commit to, in order to develop the performance mind-set.

Performance mind-set skills	Actions I will take now
Example: not trying too hard	*Example: I am going to become aware of how hard I am trying and make sure that I maintain a feeling of softness in my shoulders and grip and keep a consistent and rhythmical swing, especially when the score is close.*

What To Improve, Measure & Evaluate?

 In order to determine exactly what you want and need to improve, measure and evaluate, ask yourself the following questions:

1. What ingredients am I putting in that result in my success?
2. What ingredients am I putting in that cause me to under-perform?

In answering these questions you must look at your performance from a broader perspective and in more detail than you might have done previously. To be able to carry on doing what you were doing successfully you also need to know what you did that created your successful outcome. Equally, to identify what specifically you need to improve, you need to look at what happened before and after the specific shot that went wrong to get a better understanding of what is breaking down. For example, your opponent gets a short ball from you and hits a winner past you down the line. Saying that you lost the point because he hit a winner doesn't help you to look at your contribution to the outcome. When you say this you are only looking at the outcome and not taking care of the ingredients that made up that point. You know that you hit a short ball to your opponent but the

Understand the ingredients that create your success and then repeat them

question is: What did YOU do/think/feel that resulted in you hitting the shorter ball? You could identify a number of things that resulted in you hitting a short ball to your opponent. Here are 10 reasons, all of which are measureable, why that short ball might have happened and none of these are particularly technical:

1. Your feet weren't in the right position so you didn't get behind the ball effectively, or you miss-timed the ball (this is also an indication of poor concentration and possibly a lack of mental commitment)
2. You held your breath as you were hitting the ball (and previous shots)
3. You were distracted by something, so not focused on what you wanted
4. You were physically tight and mentally stressed
5. You were frustrated with an earlier shot in the rally
6. You missed an opportunity to win the point earlier in the rally
7. You were trying too hard and forcing the shot, or had given up
8. You hadn't made a clear decision how to play the shot
9. You were on the back foot because of the shot your opponent played (if this is the case you will want to track back to the previous shot and all the way back to the start of the point to find the reasons you ended up in the position of hitting a short ball)
10. You didn't recover after the shot, before the short ball, because you had already decided your opponent was going to hit a winner past you

Yes, of course your opponent also did something effectively and that is why they won the point and you didn't. However, you need to look at what you did so you can learn about your own contribution to your results. If you don't do this, nothing will change and you will continue looking at your opponent or other external factors for the reasons why you lose. In looking from a broader perspective at all the ingredients you put into your performance, you are appreciating what happened mentally, emotionally, physically and physiologically rather than just the outcome.

This type of evaluation enables you to see the patterns in your performance, the things you do consistently – whether effective or ineffective. You will also see that if you do the opposite of the 10 things above you are likely to perform well! Here are two different scenarios to help you appreciate how you can look at your performance from a broader perspective and in a lot more detail. Later you will learn how to use an effective problem solving method which will help you with 'in the moment' self-evaluation.

Scenario 1 – You hit a winner down the line

You need to understand what you did to create the winning opportunity (the sequence of shots you played leading up to that final shot) and the impact you had on the opponent before you hit that winner? Did you move the opponent out wide or deep? Were they off balance? Did you get a short or slower ball back as a result of what you had done? Did you use disguise or surprise? Or did you take a big risk and hit that winner? Would you be able to repeat the situation that created the winner again and again (were you in control) or was there an element of luck involved? What was your emotional state like playing the point and the final shot? How engaged and focused in the game were you (compared to thinking about the outcome)? How hard were you trying? Did you put in more effort than was needed (muscling the ball)? Did you recover after you hit the final shot or did you assume it wasn't coming back? Did you have a mental impact on your player before you hit the winner, which meant they had given up? Had you been applying pressure through the consistency of your shot making? Had you been outrunning your opponent? Were you feeling confident in your ability to win the point by executing your plan?

Scenario 2 – The opponent hits a shot past you

What did you do that enabled them to hit the shot past you? Did you give them a short ball? Were you out of position hitting your shots? Were you feeling physically tight or mentally under pressure? Were you pushing or guiding the ball rather than hitting through your shots? How exactly did the point play out (from start to finish – looking at the impact of each shot and the result of that impact)? Did you miss an earlier opportunity in the point yourself? Did you get passive in your shot making? Did you lose focus on what you were doing? Had you given up? Was your recovery after shots poor? Were you caught out watching the line assuming the ball was out, or being critical of yourself and your shots? Were you feeling tired and not bothering to play because you had already decided you were going to lose the point or the match? What were you allowing yourself to be distracted by? Did you play an excellent point and simply lose to a player who played it more effectively than you did? Were you feeling anxious or doubtful that you would win the point?

You can see in these 2 scenarios that you are looking at a number of factors together that contributed to you achieving the end result – the outcome (whether good or bad). In order to decide what you need to improve specifically you must also understand the patterns of thoughts and emotional responses that contributed to your performance. The thought and emotional patterns that you run can cause you to be successful and the thought and emotional

Your thoughts and feelings contribute to your performance. Change them to change your results

patterns you run can cause you to make errors. You need to become aware of how your thought and emotional patterns are contributing to your results so that you can learn to think and respond effectively to create the results you want. Something is considered a pattern (either helpful or unhelpful) when you do, or think that thing often, and when you have the same emotional response to a specific situation (e.g. when you always get frustrated if you double fault). These patterns could include thoughts, such as:

- I always start slow
- I always lose the first set to players who aren't as good as me
- I always double fault at deuce point
- I always feel rushed when…
- I always feel I have to hit the ball hard…
- I always feel I have to catch up when…
- I always win from deuce

They could also include emotional responses, such as:

- I always make mistakes when feeling under pressure
- I always feel nervous when I am ahead in the game
- I always feel angry if I lose when I shouldn't
- I always love the feeling of being ahead
- I always feel more relaxed playing better players

Although the word always has been used with the statements above, the chances are that you will not 'always' do it, but you might feel as if you always do it. One thing you will notice is that I have called these patterns thought and emotional patterns. They will have been constructed by you based on: specific evidence that you have gathered as a function of your previous performances, what you have seen, what others have said to you and what you say to yourself. These thoughts become your beliefs about yourself and they can either help you to be successful or they can hold you back.

You may be asking yourself, how can I change these thoughts when they are true? The reality is that these thoughts are not 'absolutely true', although for you they may feel as if they are true. They cannot be true unless you have finished performing, because you can always change them. In other words, you may see yourself as a slow starter because you feel you have always started slow (in the past), but does that mean you always have to be a slow starter? No. Instead you can work out a more effective way of starting matches; perhaps by doing a more

Work out more effective ways to achieve your results

intensive warm up to get your heart rate up, perhaps hitting within yourself for the first few points (within yourself does not mean passive) and most definitely learning to remain calm in your mind and relaxed in your body from the start of the match? Firstly, work out what you are doing that is resulting in you starting slowly then change something. Higher levels of physical and mental activation will help, as will a clear focus on how you plan to play the first few games (your game plan) and the self-discipline to stick to it.

Below is an action plan for you to work on your mental skills for any of the thoughts and emotional responses discussed above. I hope that this will give you an idea of the things you could improve in order to perform without those limiting thoughts and emotional responses.

Thought/Emotional Response	Actions to take to improve
I always start slow	This means you are not appropriately activated, physically or mentally. So… 1. Make sure you physically warm up well, including sprints (sprints help to get rid of nerves as well as getting you pumped up) 2. Don't avoid thinking about the match as this will make you static, instead keep your mind on your plan and how you want to start the match. Remember that just because you want to start in a particular way doesn't mean that it will happen, but whether it happens or not is not the point. You must do this mental preparation if you want to start more effectively.

Thought/Emotional Response	Actions to take to improve
I always lose the first set to players who aren't as good as me	You are not focusing effectively and likely to be tight because you don't want to lose. So... 1. Be really clear about how you are going to play your opponent and do it, and expect them to play better than their rating. 2. Be confident and not careless or complacent. Just because someone isn't as good as you on paper doesn't mean they cannot play well. You have to respect that they may play well and be ready for the challenge.
I always double fault at deuce point	You are allowing anxiety to control your actions. You have to expect to feel a bit nervous at times during a match. Just makes sure you take action to control the nerves. So... 1. Do deep belly breathing as part of your routine to prepare for service. 2. Be very focused on where you are going to serve the ball and be disciplined to only hit the ball if you have tossed it in the right place.
I always feel rushed when...	If you feel rushed it is a sign of you feeling under pressure or stress. You need to control your state and focus your mind. So... 1. Deliberately slow your movements down at the back of the court, maybe stand still for 5 seconds and relax (5 seconds will feel like a long time, but it isn't). 2. Focus on what you are going to do and make sure your mind isn't predicting the results before they happen.

Thought/Emotional Response	Actions to take to improve
I always feel I have to hit the ball hard when...	Feeling the need to hit the ball hard (when it is not necessary) is a sign of anxiety about the outcome. If you trusted that how you were hitting the ball would get you the result you want you wouldn't feel the need to hit the ball any harder. It is also a sign of a lack of appreciation of what the game is about if you feel that hitting the ball hard is the only tactical weapon you have. So... 1. Be more concerned about playing the tactically appropriate shot rather than just hitting the ball hard. Sometimes direction is more important than pace. 2. Learn to back yourself and that your tactical plan will give you the best chance of success. You can only do this by doing what you say you will, assessing the outcomes and tweaking your plan for next time.
I always feel I have to catch up when...	The feeling of needing to do something different or special to catch up is again a sign that you don't trust what you are doing will get you the outcomes you want. You are too focused on the score and not focused on what you need to do to give yourself the best chance of winning. So... 1. Recognize that the flow of the match always changes and the score in any moment doesn't reflect how the match will finish, until the match has finished. 2. You must trust your plan and look to execute it with rhythm and timing, not muscle and tension. Relax and stay focused on what you want to achieve in the next point.

Thought/Emotional Response	Actions to take to improve
I always win from deuce	This is a great belief to have providing you don't get complacent. Having strong positive beliefs helps with your commitment to the shot. So... 1. Make sure you still focus on what you want to achieve with your serve. 2. Continue to learn from what you are doing mentally doing well and apply it in other areas of your game.
I always make mistakes when feeling under pressure	The feeling of pressure generally comes from a lack of certainty about the result or your abilities to create the result. So... 1. Turn doubts around by focusing more specifically on where you want the ball to go. In the court is not specific enough (unless you are a beginner). 2. When you feel under pressure do deep breathing and focus on your breath whilst relaxing your upper body and face (especially your jaw).
I always feel nervous when I am ahead in the game	Your thoughts are in the future rather than the present moment. You are thinking of potentially losing from a winning position or starting to play badly. So... 1. Take confidence from what specifically you have done, mentally and tactically to be in the lead. 2. Continue to do what you have done. Don't slacken off and don't try and do too much. Don't get too conservative. Continue to play your game – the game that got you into a winning position.

Thought/Emotional Response	Actions to take to improve
I always feel angry if I lose when I shouldn't	There really is no such thing as 'shouldn't lose'. You will lose if you play worse than your opponent and thinking of what should and should not happen is a distraction to you performing. So... 1. When you have lost and are feeling angry, be sure to work out exactly what you did that caused you to lose. What you did, not what the opponent did! Mentally and tactically, how did you lose? Be very specific. 2. Commit to rectifying your errors in your next match against someone who is not as good as you. Make sure if you lose to them again you do so playing well.
I always love the feeling of being ahead	Excellent, this is a great skill to have. Make sure that you continue to maintain your lead and don't give away cheap points. Learn to be clinical in your performance as this is a very professional quality. So... 1. Keep doing what is getting you success and keep one eye out for changes in momentum so that you also continue to respond, rather than getting caught out. 2. Stay focused and continue to drive forwards, don't slacken off or get complacent. You may need to set yourself some targets to go for that keeps you focused and engaged.
I always feel more relaxed playing better players	This is clearly because you have nothing to lose (both in terms of ratings and in your mind), which means you are not feeling any pressure. This is a mental cop out! What happens if you get into a winning position? How relaxed do you feel? So... 1. Always give yourself the best chance of winning no matter who you are playing against and then you won't be surprised when you get into a winning position. 2. Learn to manage your emotional state so that you can handle nerves no matter who you are playing against, rather than allowing the person you are playing to influence you so much.

You will notice that there are some common actions you can take to solve the problems that you encounter on the court. Breathing effectively and focusing only on what you want to achieve are two of the key mental skills you need to do well. The challenge is in you developing the discipline (another key mental skill) to do those things time and time again. Use your pre-point routines to stabilize your emotional state and to focus your attention. Tennis lends itself to this well because there are lots of stops and starts in the game and lots of opportunities to get yourself back on track. There is no reason for you to wait until the end of a game or a set to get back in the game. You can get back in it at every single point, if you take the right action.

Always look for and appreciate the patterns that get you success, the things you do well, so that you can repeat them. It is too easy to look for the things you are not doing well and this can be very destructive to your confidence over time. Remember, if you can repeat something time and time again, you must be doing it well, even if what you are doing doesn't get you the results you want! So if you are not getting the result you want change one of the ingredients and you will change your results.

Task...

Now identify some of your thought and emotional patterns and have a go at coming up with some things that you can do to help you to think or feel differently, which will change your outcomes.

Thought/Emotional Response	Actions to take to improve

Beliefs Impact Performance

 Whatever you believe is possible, or not possible, for you to achieve you can easily create for yourself. The belief cycle in Figure 1 below shows you how our beliefs work and why this is the case.

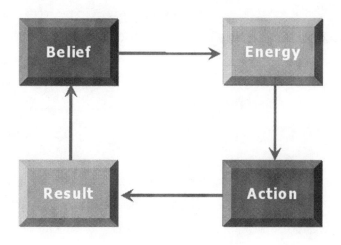

Figure 1. The Cycle of Beliefs

Your beliefs become a self-fulfilling prophecy unless you challenge them because whatever you believe you can or cannot achieve influences the energy you put in and the action you take. This in turn affects the results you get (which is your evidence), which then reinforces your belief! If you believe you can do something you will put in loads of energy, take as much action as you need to and get the results you want, which reinforces your belief that you can do it. If on the other hand you believe you cannot do it, you will put in less energy, less action and get worse results, which reinforces your belief that you cannot do it.

If you have already started to take action doing the tasks in this program and not seen the results you want yet, you may start to believe that this doesn't work and if you do that you will soon stop doing the work that you need to do. Remember that the changes you are making require significant repetition in the same way your physical skills do, in order for you to become really good. Maintaining a positive belief will keep you focused and engaged in the process of learning and developing your skills for longer, and that will lead you to achieve more success than if you quit before seeing the benefits of the work you are doing.

Our beliefs can be helpful and unhelpful under different circumstances. For example, if you believe that you cannot beat a player it may help you by taking some of the pressure off you to win, which may result in you feeling more relaxed and free to play. It may also give you the opportunity to focus really well on the process of tennis rather than the outcomes. But this belief may also limit you in terms of your potential achievements because you are not backing yourself from the start, so you are not learning to handle the pressure and may struggle to finish off the game if you do take the lead.

When we have very strong beliefs (especially about ourselves) we can be resistant to changing them. We may also feel strong negative feelings when these beliefs are challenged. When our beliefs aren't that strong we can change them easily and our feelings remain positive or neutral. This is because, technically speaking, we don't have as much mental and emotional energy invested in a weak belief as we do in a strong belief.

The level of importance we give to something raises the energy we invest in our beliefs, which can result in us feeling bad if important things we think should happen, don't happen. For example, believing you should get into a specific tennis event that is important to you and finding out that you haven't is going to feel more of a let down than not getting into an event that isn't important to you.

We are also inclined to have stronger beliefs for the things that we can be certain about. For example, believing you can win the match because the person you are playing against is no-where near your playing standard would be a strong belief to hold. This belief is strong only because you think the outcome is a virtual certainty. When this belief is seriously threatened though, as when you start losing when you should in your mind be winning, the negative

> *Beliefs can help you achieve or they can hold you back. Either way they will be true...*
> *for you*

feelings you experience can be very strong and significantly inhibit your performance.

So, the strength of the belief you hold can easily influence the strength of your emotional response as well as the amount of effort you put in. Strong beliefs can be very helpful, but they can also hold you back because of the strength of negative emotions that you may experience when they are challenged. You need to be able to take control of your beliefs so that you can maintain an appropriate peak performance state.

As I have mentioned, positive beliefs held strongly, such as 'I should win the match' can be very helpful, but they can also really backfire if you start losing the match because the negative feeling you get when you start losing can really inhibit your performance. One of the ways to handle this situation is to have, what I would call, an emotionally balancing belief. An emotionally balancing belief is where the opposite belief is also acceptable to you, rather than being something you want to avoid. Please notice that I have said acceptable rather than desirable. I am not saying that you need to want to lose the match, what I am saying is that you need to be 'okay' with the fact that you could lose the match rather than fearing losing the match. For example, if you believe that you should win the match but you also accept it is possible for you to lose the match, you will remain more balanced throughout the match rather than responding negatively if the score goes against you.

Learning to hold strong beliefs whilst also being flexible by accepting other outcomes are also possible is a great way to stay calm. When you stay calm it is easier to stay focused. Staying calm and focused are two great mental skills to master. Please remember though that, accepting other possibilities as outcomes and staying calm doesn't mean that you stop moving your feet, stop focusing and stop working to achieve the outcomes you want!

Task...

Identify some of your strong beliefs and how you would feel if they were challenged. Then for each of the strong beliefs work out what else you need to believe to lessen any negative response you would feel if your belief is challenged.

My strong beliefs?	How I would feel if the belief was challenged	What I also need to believe to lessen a negative response when challenged?

Thoughts, Emotions, Behaviors

Your thoughts and emotions (moods) lead to your specific behavioral patterns and responses. Behavioral patterns are where you run the same behaviors, such as: the same warm up pre-match, the same routine during a match, the same responses and reactions at pressure points or the same responses to being challenged. How you are thinking and feeling in any moment will have an impact on the quality of your behaviors and therefore your results. What you are thinking and how you are feeling can easily result in you changing a behavior resulting in a different outcome. For example, when you are feeling positive you do a great pre-game warm up routine and get fully focused for the match. Yet, when you feel negative or flat you don't bother with a warm up at all, or if you do it you don't engage in it fully. Your approach to your game has changed as a function of what you are thinking and how you are feeling.

The thoughts and feelings that you have when you make mistakes will also influence how you subsequently perform. When you make mistakes it is most common to look for a technical problem to solve, so your thoughts could be directed to finding a technical solution. Then if you try to work out what is going wrong but can't solve the problem, you could find yourself getting frustrated or even giving up. Negative emotions will always damage your performance. You may be able to blast a couple of winners in the heat of rage or frustration, but you will not be able to maintain this approach over the course of a match and your performance will deteriorate. This deterioration can happen dramatically or slowly and progressively. The thoughts you are having will influence the speed of collapse you experience.

Negative emotions will always damage your performance

Taking control of your thoughts is a challenge you must master if you are going to mentally support yourself to perform to your highest potential. When you take on the challenge of controlling your thoughts the first thing you will notice is that you keep having the same thoughts return to your mind. This is perfectly normal because your thoughts are also a habit. They are a habitual way of responding to the situation you have just experienced. The way to deal with this is to put those unhelpful thoughts onto a cloud and have them pass you by. If you give them your energy (by repeating them, focusing on them or worrying about them), you will make them stronger and they will destroy your performance. If, instead, you firstly recognize that you are having the thought then put it onto a cloud and replace it with a more helpful thought, you will give yourself the best chance of performing well. Some key phrases that you need in your bag, together with examples of when you would use them are given below:

- **'Maybe'** – this is a great word to use when you have thoughts that are around certainty or negativity. So the thought 'I am going to lose' would be changed to 'maybe I will lose and maybe I won't'. This is a more helpful thought to have than 'I am going to lose'. Notice how different that thought feels.

- **'Sometimes'** – this is a great word to use instead of 'always' or 'never'. If you think you 'always' or 'never' do something it doesn't leave you with much of a chance to change because these terms are very black and white and extreme. 'Sometimes' sits in the middle and helps you to move away from an extreme. Remember even a positive 'always', such as 'I always win at this event' can backfire on you.

- **'It depends'** – everything depends, nothing is certain. You need to learn about the conditions or circumstances in which things work or don't work.

- **'I can'** – is a more helpful thought than 'I will' because it is about your potential rather than certainty. 'I will' is suggesting there is certainty and that may not be the case.

- **'I want to'** – is a more helpful thought to hold than 'I should', or 'I have to'. When you say I should or I have to you are putting pressure on yourself and basically saying that if you don't achieve you are failing. As in, 'I have to…or else!'

Essentially, to manage your thoughts, and subsequently your emotional responses, you must use the words that that soften the blow when things don't go as you planned. You will need to create a diary of these so that you commit them to your memory and make them a positive habit. Using these terms will help you to you stay focused and in emotional control.

Task...

Identify some of your unhelpful thoughts and then come up with some words that you can use instead to manage your emotional responses

My unhelpful thoughts are?	Words I can use instead are?
Example: I should beat this player because he is not as good as me.	Example: I can beat this player if I deliver my plan.

Identifying The Causes of Errors (SIMS)

 Whilst it is true that an unforced error is the result of a breakdown in technique/skills you need to ask yourself what caused the breakdown in skills in that moment in time?

If you can do something at high intensity in your training, the key factor that influences your ability to deliver the same technique/skills in a competitive performance environment is most often going to be mental. Mental errors will cause a breakdown in technique. Sometimes the cause may also be physical in nature, such as tiredness. The mental and physical are also very closely aligned, since you can override your physical condition (such as tiredness) through using the power of your mind and you can also make yourself feel more tired than you really are through the power of your mind. You will remember the epic match at Wimbledon in 2010 that went on for 11 hours and 6 minutes, over 3 days, between John Isner and Nicolas Mahut, with both players repeating the same patterns of play over and over again. It was as if both players were stuck in a rut, unable to put anything more into their game, hanging on by doing what they knew they could do consistently well, leaving them in a deadlock situation. Both mentally over-riding their physical exhaustion in order to get them through to the end of the day, hoping the next day would give them renewed strength. Of course, such a challenge takes its toll and it is no surprise that both players ended their tournament as a result of this match. We all have mental and physical limits of tolerance that will be related to how well we have trained our skills. The question you have to answer is, are you developing your mental and physical skills to achieve success at the highest level of pressure, or are you losing the plot in your training?

I designed this simple effective process you can follow to evaluate the causes of errors whilst working with elite tennis players and coaches at an International High Performance Centre. I have called this process **SIMS**, which is an acronym for: State, Intention, Movement & Skills. The reason we don't look at technical causes first is because unless you are in a great emotional and physiological state, with the right intention (mind-set) and moving effectively your technique will suffer and your game will break down.

State – The first place to start any evaluation of your performance is your emotional and physiological state. You have to be in an effective 'performance state' to play well. If you are not, your technique can easily break down and you are more likely to make unforced errors in a match that you

Your emotional and physiological state is the key cause of unforced errors

wouldn't do in training. Ask yourself, were you in a positive, engaged and appropriately calm state? If not this is an area you will need to work on. You need to learn what an appropriate state is for you. That is to say the right balance of calmness and intensity and the right balance of tension that is appropriate for you to execute your shots effectively and the right balance of relaxed effort. As a general principle, negative emotions, over excitement and excessive tension or 'trying too hard' will get you out of the performance state and you will underperform. If you are too fired up be sure to practice meditation and deep belly breathing to calm you down. If you are too laid back make sure you exert yourself physically to get your heart rate up a bit, to get activated.

Intention – This is the second place to look and this is about what you intended to do to achieve your tactical plan. Did you have a strong tactical intention or were you just trying to beat the opponent? Were you playing through habit which means you didn't really have any particularly focused intention? Were you just hitting and hoping that your opponent would make a mistake? Were you intending to stay relaxed and calm? Were you

Your intentions drive your fous of attention

intending to play smart or finish early? Were you intending to follow your objectives or had you forgotten them? Were you intending to work hard or had you mentally or physically given up? You need to be clear about the differences between thinking, awareness and appropriate focus. Thinking at the wrong times will block your performance, awareness is essential for you to learn and problem solve and an appropriate focus is on the task at hand, not outcomes or results. Your intention is effectively a mental commitment to what you are doing that drives your focus of attention and your actions.

Without that commitment you will always defer to your habitual response, which is likely to be driven by the score or outcome and this will result in you feeling more tension and pressure.

Movement – If your state was great and you had the right intentions for your performance the next place to look at is your movement. Did you recover from the previous shot and then get set behind the ball before it bounced? Were you appropriately aligned with the ball? Did you read the

Move, move, move. And make sure you know the right places to recover to!

game and create the space? Were you fluid with your movements and covering the ground effectively? If your movement was not effective you need to have the intention (mental commitment) to get it right and then just do it, or practice the movement skill if you need to develop it further first.

Skills – If you were in a great state, your intentions were right and you were moving well but still making errors, this is the time to look at your technique. In a performance environment (a match), however, you would not want to be making technical changes. Instead you would rely on the skills you have in that moment and work on delivering your state, intentions and movement, including your intention to make the shot happen even if you are out of position.

Any technical problems identified in your performance should be taken back to the training environment and worked on there. The main reason for this is that there is too much that can go wrong technically and your ability to technically problem solve within a competitive performance will be limited. Trying to resolve technical problems further inhibits your performance as it removes you from the requirements of performance, such as the performance mind-set and focusing on what you want to achieve, and instead it has you thinking about what is going wrong and getting frustrated. Too much technical thinking is also a major cause of

If you think too technically you may suffer with choking at critical points in the match

choking and freezing responses, (which is an involuntary muscle tension that will inhibit your performance of fine motor skills).

One way this technical problem solving can be overcome is through the use of 'technical cues'. These simple cue words, such as 'toss', 'reach', 'snap' are there to remind you of a feeling or aspect of the technical skill that keeps you focused, without leading you into technical problem solving mode. However, for technical cues to be effective they first have to be trained so that you learn that the cue word you use leads to the behavior you want and the outcome you want. So if you have the cue word 'toss'

Technical cues help you to stay focused without disrupting your performance

to remind you to toss your ball in a specific place, you have to know what that place is and that if you deliver the ball toss in that place it will lead to you achieving more success with your serve. The cue word becomes anchored to a positive outcome, which means that you will use the cue word to stay focused or recover your focus in the match.

Task...

Remember... use **SIMS** – State, Intention, Movement, Skills (cue words) to problem solve during a match. Firstly, though, practice **SIMS** in your training, even if you are learning new techniques, work with **SIMS**. You will learn your technical skills more effectively if you are in the right state with the right intention and you are moving well! Identify what are your common errors? Is it your state, your intention, your movement or your skills? Commit to working to develop these skills.

Make a list of the technical cues that you use to keep you focused on the right things during a game. For example, when I serve I think 'reach' as this gives me the best chance of getting on top of the ball.

Aspect of the technique	Cue word
Example: Serve	Example: Reach

Working On What You Have Identified

There are 3 components or processes in the development of any skill. These are known as: teaching, training and performing. The teaching element takes place when the skill is not known and has to be taught, whether that skill is mental, physical, tactical or technical. The training element happens after the skill has been taught and the objective is to further develop the skill through repetition and under increasing degrees of difficulty and pressure. The performance element is about you taking what you have learned and trained to the competitive arena and performing it under competitive conditions (the higher levels of perceived stress).

When monitoring your outcomes in a competitive environment it is easy to see that something technical has broken down, but there are some questions you need to ask before deciding how to solve this problem. The first question to ask is: "Can I deliver this in training at a level of intensity that is

Make sure your training is more intense and challenging than your performance

equivalent to the performance?" In other words are you able to execute a level of mastery – for example, achieving the outcome 8 or 9 times out of 10, over and over again, whilst feeling under some pressure. If the answer is "yes" the problem you have is most likely to be down to how you are handling competitive pressure and the solution is therefore to develop your mental skills to handle the situation. Before answering this question though, you must be clear as to how 'trained' your skills are. Poorly formed skills will not stand up under match conditions, which means you may think you are more capable than you really are! Virtually every player I have profiled has said that their training is less intense and more relaxed than when they compete, which simply means that their training is ineffective in preparing them for a competitive arena. Your training environment should feel more intense than when you are competing.

If you cannot do something in training you have to ask yourself if you know how to do it? If the answer is "no" then you need to be taught how to do it. Remember that being taught how to do a skill (mental, physical, tactical and technical) does not make you competent at delivering that skill on the court. Thinking you have the skill when it is not fully formed (through effective training) is a mistake a lot of players make and results in a great deal of frustration when they cannot perform it well in competition.

If you know how to do it, then the answer is that you need to train the skill – to form the skill. Training the skill is necessary to achieve levels of mastery under pressure. It requires that you push the limits of your comfort, especially physically and mentally. In essence you are trying to maintain the quality of your strokes and outcomes whilst replicating the stresses that would be experienced on the match court, through other challenges, such as movement, rally tolerance, increasing difficulty of ball characteristics received (more spin or pace, directional challenges etc), tiredness, concentration lapses and emotional stresses. This type of training is often associated with the 'Spanish way', the power of which, in developing mental resilience, should not be under-estimated. Skills that are well trained stand up under the pressure of competitive performance, which gives you the edge over players who have less well trained skills. When you know you have trained your skills well, you will be able to achieve higher levels of competitive performance and build greater confidence based on your increasing levels of competence.

If you are unable to identify what specifically you need to work on, you will need to seek the advice of professional experts in each of the areas of development: mental, technical, tactical and physical. Working on the wrong thing will make your progress slower and at worst can limit your ability to achieve your highest potential in the sport.

Task...

Identify how your game has broken down (be sure to get to all the ingredients and not just the technical skill) and then whether you need to be taught something, train something or work on your mental skills to be able to perform more effectively?

What in my game caused me to make the error?	What do I need to learn or train?
Example: my forehand broke down because I didn't recover effectively after the shot before.	*Example: I know how to recover and where to recover to, but my concentration was not on the game. I need to train myself to stay focused until the point is over.*

Considering Your Long Term Development

Your developmental program to become a great performer is not determined simply by how you competed in your last performance. You must also consider your long-term development and what is needed for you to be able to compete in the future, at a different/higher level. If you only consider the short term, you may never get to your long-term goal. Equally, if you never consider the short term you may get frustrated or bored and opt out before you can get to achieve your long-term goal.

In considering what is required for your longer term development you are likely to need to take specialist advice in all areas of the game: technical, tactical, mental and physical. Many great players fail to achieve their potential because they have not considered the requirements in the longer term when working on their development for their performance tomorrow. Your mental skill development is particularly important in this respect because any bad habits you learn in the short term will have to be changed for you to achieve your long term objectives and we know the process of changing habits is a painful one!

As a general principle, it is thought that very young and new performers need to develop their technique as a priority whilst also making sure that they are able to compete and stay free from injury. Whilst this is of course true, it is also true that the mental skills are being developed from the time we are born, so by the time a player starts playing tennis, they will already have some good and bad mental habits that need to be managed and developed. A performer who already has well developed technique may still have to consider technical development in order to enable them to deliver specific higher level tactical outcomes and also to prevent injury. However, a program that is heavy on technical development and light on the other areas will be out of balance and result in under-achievement in the longer term. Each element (technical, tactical, physical and mental) has its foundational elements, the absence of which will always limit the achievement of peak performance. In other words, there are some basic standards in all areas of development that must be achieved for players to be able to achieve their optimum competitive performance. You are working on some of the key foundational mental skill elements throughout this program and specifically those skills that will help you to feel more confident.

> *Seek specialist advice in respect of the long-term development of skills*

A program that does not consider the appropriate mental or physical development of the performer also has the potential to cause physical and psychological injury. In performance terms, poor physical and psychological development is the equivalent of taking away a technical/tactical weapon from a player. Imagine playing without your forehand. You would feel very constrained and soon lose enjoyment for the sport. An appropriately designed program should therefore ensure that players feel they are growing and expanding all their skills and continuing to enjoy competing at the highest level possible.

Increasing Intensity
& Stress

You need to be able to comfortably operate at increasing levels of intensity and stress in order to improve and achieve the highest levels of performance you are capable of in the game. Intensity can be technical, physical, mental or emotional. Players in general prefer or can relate to physical intensity because they usually feel great for a physical workout. But intensity must also come with quality otherwise all the great exercise you do is being undermined by poor technique or mental intention and will not help you in the competitive arena. If you are someone who feels that their training is not as intense and stressful as the competition itself you need to find ways to increase the intensity of your training. The use of multi-sensory visual imagery, to experience stress before engaging in a training session or specific drill, should be part of your mental skills development. Remember that you have already practiced multi-sensory imagery with the lemon example when we looked at how the mind and body are intricately linked.

A very simple way to increase the feeling of stress in your training is to imagine a situation that caused you to feel stressed, nervous, anxious or angry in the past. As you think of that time, imagine that it is happening right now by seeing the things that happened, hearing the sounds and you will find that the feelings you had back then return to you now. As soon as you feel those feelings you can continue with your training.

Take control of what you can control and let go of what you cannot control

In doing this you are teaching yourself to handle the feelings of nerves, anxiety, anger, etc. When you feel the feelings of course, you cannot just continue to play. You must in that moment of feeling learn to deep breathe effectively and train your mind to focus on the task.

Within your training, pressure can also be applied through challenging your: movement, thinking, problem solving, decision making, mental processing, increasing the challenge technically, the use of scores, targets (such as goals to achieve) and points based challenges. As a general principle, if you are achieving a ratio of about 7 out of 10, in what you are doing, you should be moving to a higher level challenge. If you are achieving 8 or more out of 10 the challenge is too easy and less than 6 out of 10 the challenge may be too difficult. Of course at the start of any new task the challenge is going to be more difficult, but you should be able to make progress quickly, providing you are following the instructions you are given and you stay engaged in what you are doing. Where you have 100% control over what you are doing, such as with the mental skills, you should aim to achieve 100%. You can easily train your mind to not be influenced by your opponent, but you cannot train your body to not be influence by your opponent because they are going to make you move and vice versa.

The stronger, fitter and more technically skillful you are the less you will be influenced physically and technically, but your opponent is always going to have some impact. With your mind, you do have more of a choice about whether you let your opponent influence you or not. You have the potential to have 100% control over your thoughts, your emotions and how you react and respond to what happens on the court. Imagine how tough it is playing someone who, no matter what you do or say, doesn't respond to you. They just carry on, highly focused and doing the things they need to do to give themselves the best chance of success, almost as if you didn't exist. We would probably label that person as 'ice cold' or 'nerves of steel'. These are not special qualities that people are born with, they are trained skills that these players have worked hard to develop. The choice is yours – you too can become mentally tough in this way.

Where you do not have 100% control over the outcome (such as winning) 100% may not be a good target, since your success is not totally down to you! Remember, also that you cannot have 100% control over your technical or physical delivery unless your mind is supporting you! Whatever targets you set you should be striving for continuous improvement. There is no end to your potential, and if you think there is you will stop learning or working at it.

Task...

Identify the ways in which you need to increase your intensity in training in order to perform more effectively then commit to it.

I am going to increase the intensity in my training by doing the following:

Handling

Performance Stress

The difference between training and performing is easily under estimated. Some people respond really well to the performance environment and they even perform at a better level than when they train. Others struggle to perform as well as they train. In both cases, the difference is down to how the player is handling perceived stress. A player who performs well is using the stress and intensity of the competitive arena as a positive driving force, directing their concentration and energy into achieving the outcomes they want. Players who struggle in competition are using that energy against themselves, often more concerned about not losing than achieving the outcomes they want. Learning to direct your perceived stress to drive your performance in a positive way is essential for you to achieve your highest potential.

The key to achieving this skill is in part down to your self-discipline. You can either allow yourself to be distracted by your thoughts and feelings or you can adopt the following strategy to help you channel your energy effectively:

1. Acknowledge your feelings (don't bury them)
2. Be okay with the feelings of nerves and anxiety – see them as your body firing you up and getting you ready to perform
3. Learn to see all points as the same level of importance rather than thinking in terms of big points and critical points, which will only add to your stress
4. Focus on what you want to achieve and use deep breathing to help with reducing the feelings – build this into your routine
5. Say positive, supportive and helpful things to yourself and use words such as 'maybe'

Task...

Identify whether you are someone who uses performance stress to focus your concentration and energy into achieving the outcomes you want, or someone who worries more about losing?

Now, if you are someone who could improve your performance by channeling performance stress, remember that deep belly breathing will help you to deal with any anxiety. You simply need the discipline to do deep breathing to over-ride any negative or destructive thoughts and focus your attention on what you want to achieve. When you are belly breathing remember to keep your focus on your breath. This takes practice and discipline. So please, now, commit to working hard on belly breathing and your focus so that you can perform more effectively in the future.

Declaration of Commitment

I ......Josh Tyler Reynolds...... commit to working hard to develop the skills of belly breathing and focus my attention on what I want to achieve (tactically) and not allow myself to be distracted when I don't get the outcomes I want.

Signed ......R..

Dated ......10/3/14..

The Cycle Of Learning

It is important to recognize the psychological and physical processes that you are going through as you learn, because the learning process influences the quality of the output that you are likely to achieve. Appreciating the cycle that you are going through as you learn and become proficient at your skills will enable you to better manage your expectations and be more confident that what you are experiencing is perfectly natural.

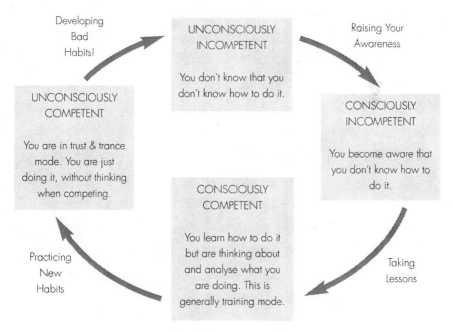

Figure 2. The Cycle of Learning

You will see in the Cycle of Learning presented in Figure 2 above, that as you are going through the stages of learning you are moving around the cycle from a stage of 'unconsciously incompetent' through to 'unconsciously competent'.

There are consequences for your performance at each stage. At the stage of being unconsciously incompetent you don't know that you cannot do something, or you don't know that you don't know how to do it. This may be because you have never been taught the skill, or it may be that you have old or bad habits in relation to that skill. For example, you may have never been taught the specific movement patterns for a shot, but you have your own way of moving to hit the ball. If your own way involves movement habits that are ineffective and you are not aware that your movement is ineffective then you are unconsciously incompetent in this respect. Remember that you may also be at this stage of unconsciously incompetent in respect of your mental skills in that you may not realize that what you are thinking is not effective!

Raising you awareness is critical for your continued learning & success

When the coach raises your awareness to the fact that your movement is ineffective, you become consciously incompetent – you are aware that what you are doing doesn't work very well. In learning the new movement pattern, which you will do as you progress around the cycle through to unconscious competence, you are also unlearning your old pattern of movement. In effect, you are running a new neural pathway to create a new movement and over-ride the old one. But you need to create a really strong pathway for the change to become permanent. If you do not train the new pattern to the level of unconscious competence, the old pattern will be the easiest for you to do (it will have the most neural connections to it), and the one you are most likely to revert to under pressure. So under pressure you may become consciously incompetent again which means you are aware that you are doing your old movement and not the new one. Or you may remain unconsciously incompetent if you are not aware that you are doing your old movement pattern.

To get the best out of your training and learn new skills you need to keep your awareness raised. If you train with low awareness it would be very easy for you to become unconsciously incompetent and then you are always dependent on your coach to remind you that you are not doing the new movement pattern (which they cannot do during a match). What is very important though is that you do not beat yourself up as you raise your awareness. Some players feel that knowing they are getting it wrong somehow means they are not being successful, but this could not be further from the truth. Think about it; would you rather go on in blind ignorance thinking that you are doing really well (when you are not), or would you rather know exactly how well you are doing so that you can take action to improve and get to the level that you want to achieve?

Knowing what you need to do and doing it are two different things. The first step in the process of learning is awareness and you are likely to become aware of a lot of things that you could do better. Just because there are a lot of things you could do better doesn't make you a failure. On the contrary, it means you are aware of the opportunities there are for you to improve. From this position of awareness you can take action to develop your skills and achieve higher levels of competence. So please don't get into the bad habit of beating yourself up because you feel you know what you need to do but you are not doing it. You are likely to always know or be aware of more than you

Knowing and doing are different things. You cannot 'do' without 'knowing' and you cannot improve without 'doing'

act on. That is human nature. Take strength from knowing what you need to do and then take confidence from taking the action to change. With awareness your learning will be greater and your transformation quicker.

When you are at the stage of 'consciously incompetent' you realize you can't do it very well. You may need some help raising your awareness and your coaches and mental skills expert are there to help you. So you begin to take lessons and during that time you will be thinking a great deal about what you are doing. As a result of this thoughtful process you are becoming 'consciously competent'. But because you are thinking a lot, in order to remember to do the right things to improve your skills, your performance can suffer. Initially, in the learning of new movement skills, your movement is going to be slower than when you are able to do the skill without thinking. This can be a challenging time for you mentally, but you should take confidence from the fact that if you continue with your lessons and continue to practice hard at the right things you will eventually become 'unconsciously competent' at that skill.

The act of becoming unconsciously competent leads you to be able to play without thinking about what you are doing. That is not to say that you should play without thinking at all! You will still need to use thought cues to remind you to do certain things as you continue to improve your game and your skills. You also need to think about your tactical plans and sticking to your objectives, but this is not the same as the thinking that disturbs your performance when you are taking lessons or receiving and processing instructions. This latter thinking interrupts your natural body movements because it is about how you do the skills.

When you are at stage 3, consciously competent, you will be in a thinking state. That is often the toughest state for performing. This is because the sort of thinking you need to do in this stage will keep you out of the trancelike state that is necessary for you to perform at your best. At stage 4, unconsciously competent however, you will be able to get into this trance, which is known as 'the zone' or 'peak performance state' or 'peak state'. This zone or peak state is the ideal state for performing. Now think about the impact of this: if you find yourself thinking the wrong things in a match, trying to work out how to correct your technique or criticizing yourself for not achieving what you wanted to, how is this going to affect your ability to remain in a peak state? This type of thinking is not going to help you get into the peak state and will result in you under-performing. But remember that conscious competence is a stage you have to go through. The more focused you are the quicker you will get through it.

Sometimes you may deliberately decide to play a match whilst thinking a lot about what you are doing, because this gives you the best chance of improving in the longer term. The reason this is the case is very simply that until you are unconsciously competent (which requires you to go through the thinking stage) it is easy for you to slip back to the stage of unconscious incompetence. In other words, slip back into the bad habits you had before you started with your lessons. So there is a case for you playing

Thinking a lot about what you are doing doesn't mean you will lose, but it makes your task more challenging

some matches with a lot of thinking as you are transitioning your skills into the stage of unconscious competence and this shouldn't just be done in training. In order for you to do this successfully, you will need to let go of the outcome of the match and the best place to start to do this is in practice matches during your training or matches that don't mean a great deal to you. This doesn't mean that you will lose the match because you are thinking a lot during your performance, nor should you go into the match thinking that you will lose. What it does mean is that you have to play without any expectations, because you are putting your development ahead of the result.

If you are too fearful to do this because your performance might be negatively affected remember that fear results in slower progress and blocks you from achieving your highest potential. You have to learn to be comfortable facing your fears and doing what you need to do no matter how you are feeling. To stay on top of your game and to continue to create great habits for success you need to be constantly raising your awareness and working your way around this learning cycle.

At stage 4, unconscious competence, it is possible for you to move in one of 3 directions. It is possible to exit the loop in relation to this skill because it is learned and needs no further attention. It is possible to move to unconscious incompetence if you don't realize what you are doing has gone back to your old habit (which is possible under increasing stress or when a skill is not fully developed) and it is possible to move to conscious incompetence, which means you are aware that you have drifted back to an old way of doing things.

Whether we truly exit the learning cycle is often debated, since the science behind the unlearning of a skill (physical or mental) is complex and not as simple as it first seems looking at the learning cycle. If we have a way of doing the skill that is not perfect, this will be our old habit to be unlearned. For example, as a child we all learn to walk. We do this naturally and for the most part without assistance. So, as we grow up we develop a way of walking and

Our habits are ingrained in our neurology. The longer you do a habit the stronger it gets

holding our posture. If we then learn to adopt a more appropriate posture and gait (way of walking) to enable us to walk more effectively and efficiently, we will have old patterns of walking and standing to over-ride. The same is true for all our thinking patterns and emotional response patterns. We will have to think about what to do a lot in order to over-ride those old patterns. If we do not train our new posture well enough at some point our old way of walking will return and the longer you have been walking and standing with a lazy gait and posture the quicker it will return. Why? Because your old walking habit is engrained in your neurology and is therefore the easiest for you to do without thinking.

So, don't be surprised if you have to be reminded at some point in the future that an old pattern has returned. This is the constant process of change. Remember there is no end... just the process of continuous improvement. The more aware you are, the quicker you will realize if you are drifting back into an old habit and be able to get yourself back on track. The reality is very simple. If you don't think you can change something you won't change it. If you think something is possible to change then you will put in the effort to change it. I believe permanent change is possible to achieve, but the factors that are necessary for that change to take place are complex and psychological in nature... and involves far more than hitting thousands of tennis balls in the vein hope that something sticks!

Task...

Identify skills where you still need to think about how to do them (consciously competent). Then make sure your training takes the consciously competent skills to the level of unconscious competence through focused practice. If not those skills will not be developed and you will find yourself with bad habits.

Skills that I still have to think about to get them right are...

The Cycle Of Change

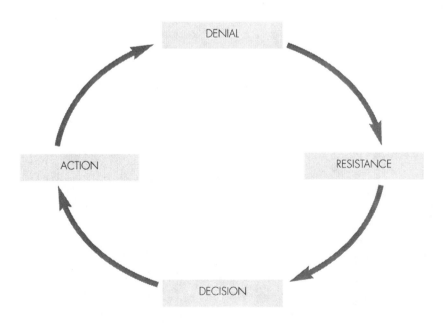Change is something most people are uncomfortable with, but it is something you need to get used to if you are going to progress and achieve your highest potential. The process of change is outlined in Figure 3 below so that you can appreciate what you may experience when making changes in any aspect of your development.

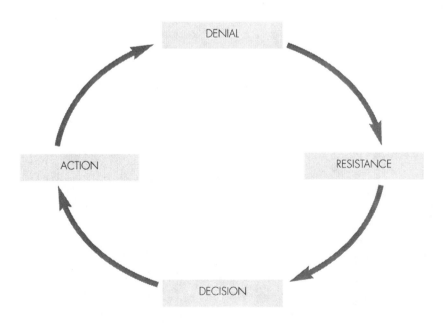

Figure 3. The Cycle of Change

Allowing yourself to move through the stages of denial and resistance as quickly as possible will enable you to change quickly. One way to do this is to always say "yes" to a challenge, even if you feel you want to say "no". Make sure any evidence you have for saying no is not governed by a limiting belief you are following. Always check with yourself when you want to say no, is it possible that what you are being asked to change could work more effectively than what you are currently doing? And if the answer to that question is "yes" or "I don't know", then accept any discomfort, be brave and make that change work for you. Remember, if you go into making any changes with a belief that what you are doing won't work you will easily be able to prove yourself to be correct. You can easily make something not work and it can be much tougher to make something work, because it requires more effort to make it work than to make it not work.

Here are some of the symptoms of denial and resistance and what you will need to do to shift yourself through the process of change when you get to the decision point and taking action:

Denial
- Feeling stuck
- Keep going round in circles – doing the same thing
- Others point out things about ourselves we don't agree with
- Failure or unwillingness to accept we need to change
- Experience aches, pains, illnesses and injury
- Dysfunctional emotional reactions and behaviors

Resistance

- Intense negative emotions such as irritation, anger and frustration – extreme and irrational although you may not feel that you are being irrational or extreme!
- Shutting off emotions – not feeling anything
- Confusion – avoidance of decisions, not knowing what to do
- Comfort zone – wanting to stay in your comfort zone
- Confidence – needing certainty, lack of faith
- Control – feeling out of control – you have to let go of control to get control

Decision

- Pain – accept the feeling of being out of your comfort zone
- Vision – focus on going for your goal
- Passion – having the desire to do what it takes to get there

Action

- Let go of the past – take action from where you are now
- Manage your mind, energy and emotions – control what you can control
- Change how you see yourself – work in your mind from your goal state
- Social group – surround yourself with people who support you
- Trust and believe in yourself – irrespective of your outcomes
- Set daily objectives to achieve and put your energy behind doing them
- NO EXCUSES or REASONS for not doing something

Many people fear change. Sometimes they can think they fear failure or even fear success when what they really fear are the changes that come with success or the changes they would have to make to prevent themselves from failing. Our desire for things to remain the same is a strong one because we need to feel safe and secure and yet the reality is that we are changing all the time. You need to learn to balance the amount of change in your training at any point in time so that it does not become too stressful, but at the same time learn to embrace change as something positive rather than something threatening. Become aware of when you are denying or resisting something and instead say yes. Then engage in what you are doing 100%, mind and body, to make it work rather than prove it doesn't work. This is another mental skill that, when you master it, will enable you to achieve your highest potential.

> *Learning to love rather than fear change is a key to your success*

Task...

Identify things that you don't feel that you need to change or that you resist changing and then look for evidence that shows you that you could achieve a better result if you did change them. Keep a record of this evidence and make the change sooner rather than later.

Things I don't want to change or resist changing are...	Evidence that shows me it would be good to change is...
Example: I know I need to work on what I am changing with my coach when we get to points play but I don't do it - I forget it and play points	Example: The speed of change you experience is slow and your performance in matches is not improving because you are doing the same thing you have always done.

Confidence From Goal Achievement & Positive Labeling

When you feel successful only because you are achieving outcomes, such as winning, it is easy to lose confidence in yourself when you are not winning and label yourself negatively as a result. If you feel confident only when you achieve perfection you will be sabotaging your confidence, as you will feel bad when you fall short of perfection. Whilst winning provides a level of confidence it is only one factor that affects confidence. And whilst perfection is strived for by many great performers the trick is not to base your confidence on the achievement of perfection, since you will always be able to improve what you have done. Perfection is not a helpful label and effectively an illusion that will leave you feeling worse about what you are doing more often than better, because perfection cannot be achieved.

The problem with building confidence based only on whether you win or lose is that it is something you don't have 100% control over. It is also not an entirely accurate measure of technical competence. Performers who lose their confidence easily when they start losing matches or when they don't perform as well as they did at some point in the past are likely to negatively label themselves. They need to learn to work at 'building their confidence'. This is achieved by working on all the things you have covered in this program so far, through positive self-labeling and through the process of goal setting and goal achievement in Part 2.

The reason goal setting and goal achievement is so important to the development of your confidence is because it focuses your attention on the things you can control which means you are able to repeat what works, change what is not working and continuously improve all your skills. It

Winning reinforces confidence but goal achievement builds confidence

gives you the evidence you need to believe in the positive labels you want for yourself. When your measures of success are based on winning this is something you do not have full control over and it is too easy to compare your success with your opponents and this is unhelpful, because it leads you to label yourself as a loser or in other unhelpful ways. Performers who are able to maintain their confidence even when they are not performing well are performers who measure their success effectively. They live up to the positive labels they create for themselves. It is no coincidence that they are also the ones who achieve more!

So, players who are successful are always 'positively labeling' themselves rather than labeling themselves as losers, chokers or bad at competing. They are always looking for the things they do well and label themselves in ways that make them feel good. Throughout the exercises in this program you

Positively labeling yourself will help to build confidence and develop the personal characteristics of excellence

will be encouraged to label yourself as a great performer and commit to bring positive characteristics to your performance that you have full control over, such as determination, patience and smart thinking. In developing these powerful positive characteristics within yourself you will become a stronger and more confident person as well as a great performer. Below is a list of characteristics that you can draw on should you wish to:

Courageous	Respectful	Determined
Energized	Committed	Accepting
Purposeful	Intensity	Focused
Aware	Problem Solver	Confident
Attacking	Patient	Smart
Resilient	Tenacious	Competitive
Self-belief	Consistent	Open
Flexibility	Supportive (team)	Leader
Balanced	Strong	Ambitious
Self-disciplined	Calm	Tough
Excellence	Professional	Organized
Motivated	Humble	Passion

A positive label in and of itself is not enough for you to feel confident. You need to train yourself to believe in the positive label. For each of the characteristics you have chosen you need to identify the behaviors and thoughts that you will adopt, which mean that you are achieving that characteristic. For example, saying well done to others, even if they beat you would be a behavior linked to respect! It is the behaviors and thoughts that you come up with that become the goals for your performance. Here are some other examples of behaviors and thoughts:

Courageous – take on new challenges even if you are a bit nervous and make them happen. Do something when competing you have been training for, even though you are nervous of doing it in the match in case it doesn't work. Think, 'I will take on this challenge'.

Patience – waits for the right time to deliver a tactical outcome, rather than rushing or forcing the situation. Think, 'There is time, it will happen'.

Awareness – effectively evaluate your performance and have a good appreciation of how you create your outcomes. Think, 'How did I make that happen?'

Openness – discuss how you are feeling and are open to coaching information. Think, 'I am open to coaching'.

Purposeful – are able to state the reason for any actions you have taken and how those actions relate to the tactical demands of your performance (are relevant and appropriate). Think, 'For what purpose am I playing this way?'

Calm – are composed during the performance (not showing signs of panicking) and continue to demonstrate clear thinking processes. Think, 'Stay calm'.

Self-disciplined – resists temptation, do what is required for your performance and do not allow yourself to become distracted. Think, 'I am going to do this even though I don't feel like it'.

Enjoyment – demonstrates professional fun, in the achievement of your goals and objectives as well as enjoying the success of winning. Think, 'I love putting the effort in to try to do well'.

Consistency – putting the same effective ingredients into your performance every time (the right state, intentions, movements & skills). Repeatedly doing a behavior, such as routines (with the mental components of the routine). Think, 'what ingredients did I put in there that made a difference?'

Self-belief – don't doubt yourself because you make mistakes. Instead solve the problem and learn that no matter what happens you can cope with it. Think, 'I know I can do this, keep going'.

Focused – giving your attention to what you want to happen on the court and not getting distracted by what has gone wrong. Think, 'tactical plan'.

Energized – bring energy to the court and engage fully in what you are doing even when things are not going your way. Seeing things as a challenge that you are up for and never feeling defeated. Think, 'Come on, once more, push it'.

Competitiveness – not making the challenge a personal one against the opponent, instead measuring your success based on your own achievements and being self competitive within the game (in other words playing the challenge of playing the game of tennis not playing to prove you are better than the opponent). Think, 'Respect my opponent and the rules of the game'.

Problem solver – come up with solutions that keep you feeling confident and performing rather than blaming things for your outcomes. Think, 'I can solve this'.

Task...

What are the 3 main positive labels that you would like to develop in yourself and what are the behaviors/thoughts that you will commit to doing to instill those positive characteristics in yourself?

Positive Characteristics Labels	What I will do (behaviors) that will instill these characteristics in myself?

Completing Your Log-Book

You can continue the process of transforming your performance now, through action, by completing the log-book that follows. This self-assessment process takes place over 12 weeks and during that time you will use your log-book on a daily basis to monitor and evaluate your progress, developing the key mental skills for success as well as your technical, tactical and physical skills. There are a series of questions for you to answer on a daily basis that enable you to stay focused, effectively reflect on your achievements and develop positive habits to transform your performance.

Having completed the exercises in the first part of the program you will have already identified the things that you know you need to work on to improve. Knowing what to do is very helpful, but your outcomes will only change when you put into practice the things you have learned in the first part of this program. You will have a lot of useful information now that will help you understand what you are experiencing as you develop yourself as a tennis player. You also know that to be a mentally tough competitor you need to work hard now at:

- adopting a performance mind-set,
- learning to problem solve (SIMS),
- challenging yourself to learn more quickly,
- increasing the intensity of your training,
- building your confidence,
- positively labeling yourself,
- developing helpful beliefs,
- embracing change,
- taking a broader perspective in developing your tennis,
- focusing effectively on what you want, and
- becoming a tactically smarter performer.

Knowledge is not enough to transform your performance. You must put what you know into action consistently and regularly. The log-book will help guide you so that you do not try to tackle too much at once and ensure that you evaluate the action you take. To start this process, you need to identify, what the most important things are for you to work on right now? Specifically, ask yourself what mental skills you want to develop and how these will help you to perform? For example:

- Learning effective problem solving will help you to remain emotionally calm and also help you stay focused as you perform
- Becoming tactically smarter will enable you to be more effective as a performer feel more confident and stay calmer even when things aren't going your way
- Embracing the cycle of change will enable you to learn new skills quickly and progress faster than others
- Positively labeling yourself will help to build your confidence and develop excellent personal characteristics that will make you successful

- Effective goal management will enable you to see your true progress which will not only help you to feel more confident in your abilities, but it will also enable you to direct your training effectively to those things that are going to have the biggest impact on your performance
- Adopting a performance mind-set is going to help you to achieve higher levels of competitive performance more often

As a simple rule, the more effort and commitment you put into completing the log-book, the more you will get out of it. If you answer any self-evaluation with 'I don't know' you will not move forwards.

'I don't know' is not good enough. Find out!

Instead, it is better to ask yourself the question, 'how could that have happened?' In other words you are always open to the possibility that you could have done something differently in order to get the result you wanted. If you ever feel you could not have done more you may be limiting your potential. Of course there may be some days where you really couldn't have done more, in which case you should be feeling really proud of yourself, your achievements and outcomes. You must learn not to blame anything for your results, including yourself! You are human and as such you are not perfect.

Make sure that you always control those things you can control and let go of the things you cannot control – without blame or guilt. Make it your goal to learn above all else and make it your goal to raise your awareness so that you can keep improving. See all things in perspective and remember nothing is either as good or as bad as it first seems. Try and look at what you are doing as if you were your own best supportive coach and take the broadest perspective you can. You can put your performances into context by asking yourself, 'how does my performance today affect my future in 5 years time?' The answer will always be, not a great deal. So nothing should be that serious as to cause you to feel distressed. The process of learning and development should be fun and exciting, because you really don't know where you will end up. You just know that it is going to be better than when you started. Will you achieve your ultimate goal in tennis? No-one can say. Will you be a better person and player for the journey you are taking? Yes. Will you feel more confident in yourself and better able to handle life on and off the court? Yes. Will you continue to enjoy the game when others have lost interest? Yes.

Then let your journey begin…

Ideally, you want to complete the log-book on a daily basis, whether you are training, resting or competing as this will keep you in touch with what you are achieving and what you need to do in order to improve. The log-book is set out in 3 x 4 week training blocks. For each block you will have the opportunity to:

- Set tactical goals and then daily performance goal setting monitoring and evaluation followed by a training block review
- Take advantage of the additional support and some top tips to help you in the following training block
- Focus on the things that are important to you now. You will become clear about how you are measuring success, monitor your progress and stay motivated along the way

- Follow the guidance in the performance section, which involves a series of questions for you to use to evaluate and learn from your performances

By completing this log-book over 12 weeks you will easily be able to stay focused and engaged in your development. You will be able to set short-term, weekly and 4 weekly objectives to improve your performance and specifically your mental performance. Over the 12 weeks, your mental discipline and dedication will help you to develop positive habits that will transform your performance.

It is important that your goals are clear and objective as much as is possible. An easy way to check if they are is to ask yourself would someone else know what you were talking about, or would they need a further explanation to know what you were measuring? So for example, if you were to say that your goal is to hit your forehand solidly this is not easily understood and would need further explanation, such as, getting set behind the ball, maintaining the path, angle and speed of your racket through the ball. Someone else must be able to look at what you said you were going to do and be able to say how well you did it.

Objective measurement becomes more of a challenge when measuring some of the mental skills, which is why you should try as far as possible to align your mental skills with specific behaviors. This means that the achievement of the behavior is the measure of your achievement of the mental goal. Some mental skills will be measured by self-report on a scale of 1-10, so it is important that you are consistent with your self-reporting and be aware that when you level of skill goes up you will need to re-evaluate your scoring system (an 8 at one level of skill will be a 4 at a higher level of skill). It would be useful to have an agreed system of measurement for your mental skills with your coach. For something like emotional control, as a general principle if your performance deteriorates when you get frustrated or laid back, or if you adopt the 'I don't care' mentality, your emotional state will not be right. A great emotional state is one in which you are focused, activated with your feet, making tactically smart decisions and free and fluid with your swing. Tightness, pushing the ball, being too aggressive, hitting outside of yourself (such that you finish off balance), unnecessary and inappropriate risk taking, freezing as you hit the ball and becoming static with your feet are all indicators of poor emotional state control.

Please do not feel you have to set loads of goals for each area of your development. You may find that you only have two things you are working on for the week. Make sure that every week at least one of your goals is a mental goal, even if it is simply developing the characteristics that will help you build your confidence through positive labeling, as discussed above. Only set goals that are appropriate and relevant for your development now. One goal that you deliver every day is going to do more for your progress than loads of goals that you don't achieve!

You may find this process to be a bit repetitive. It is and for a good reason too. Repetition leads to discipline and habit formation and that in turn leads to excellence when you are repeating the right things. You will do a lot of repetition of your forehand or serve to achieve competence at those skills. You must also achieve a good level of repetition at goal setting and evaluation in order to get into the mental discipline required and subsequently achieve the higher levels of self esteem and confidence promised.

Setting Goals For Competing

After the training blocks there is a section on competing. This section is set out as a series of questions that you can use to effectively evaluate your performance. There are questions you need to answer before you play and then after you have played. You are encouraged to be as objective as possible in your responses and look for patterns in the things that you do, think and feel. Then, you can repeat the patterns that help you and change the ones that don't.

In your evaluation always ask the question, would this be good enough at the next level? The reason for asking this question is because it keeps you moving forwards and stops complacency, especially when playing people who aren't as good as you are. It will enable you to keep your eye on what you are going to need in the future whilst still winning today. Above all, remember to enjoy competing. This should not be a chore or distressing in any way. It should be challenging and enjoyable and provide you with an opportunity to learn and develop yourself in ways that will support you in everything that you do.

As a general principle, you will set tactical, physical and mental goals only for performance, not technical goals. Technical goals (except 'technical cues' as mentioned earlier) will inhibit your performance. Performing is a time for letting go of technical thinking and you should use the SIMS process to recover errors during your performance. One goal to set is: to stick to your tactical and mental goals, especially when feeling under pressure!

My Training Log-Book

My Personal Commitment to Success

By signing below, I, ...
am committing to following this program to transform my performance.
I am agreeing to:

- Answer the questions as honestly as I can
- Push my boundaries even if I feel resistance
- Look for patterns in my performances
- Put my learning above all else
- Reward myself for success and repeat it
- Maintain an attitude of continuous improvement

I promise to do the exercises to the best of my ability even if I don't feel like it at the time.

I commit specifically to challenge my mental skills and develop positive habits that will support me in transforming my performances now and in the future.

Signed ....Date.......................

Witnessed...Date.......................

Training Block 1

Tactical or Performance Goals

What are your main tactical or performance goals and specific outcomes or targets that you want to achieve in the next 4 weeks?

e.g. When receiving a neutral ball to take control of the middle of the court by hitting either to the right or the left of the center.

1

2

3

4

5

Goals & Outcome Targets

Now for each of the Tactical/Performance Goals you have identified on the previous page, list the Goals/Outcome Targets that you need to achieve to improve your performance.

e.g. To improve my alignment with the ball I am receiving so that I can more easily control the ball I send from the middle of the court to the left or right. My outcome target is to get my alignment and contact point right on 9 out of 10 balls.

1

2

3

4

5

Process Goals

What have you identified that you need to do in order to achieve your tactical/performance goals for the next 4 weeks? Include your measures of success.

MENTAL – e.g. I am going to stay calm when moving to the ball, especially as the rally progresses beyond 5 shots, and I will know this because I keep a good tempo on the ball and won't try and over hit the ball.

PHYSICAL – e.g. I am going to keep adjusting around the ball so that my alignment is the best it can be and I will know this because I get behind the ball before the ball has bounced.

TECHNICAL – e.g. I am going to get the right contact point in order to direct the ball to the left and right when receiving the ball down the middle of the court. My cue words for this are 'in' and 'out' for inside the ball and outside the ball.

General

How motivated are you to achieve these goals in the next 4 weeks? If you are not motivated what needs to happen for you to feel motivated?

How confident do you feel that you know what you need to achieve (process goals) in the next 4 weeks? If not what action will you take to find out what you need to achieve?

Is there anything you can think of that would stop you achieving your goals? What are you going to do to overcome any potential obstacles?

What one thing can you do to increase your chances of success in the next 4 weeks?

How can you positively label yourself? What one characteristic are you going to bring to your performance every time? e.g. smart, fighter, warrior, courageous, focused, athletic, creative… What behaviors will you adopt to achieve this characteristic? Be sure to make this characteristic a mental goal for each day!

Week 1 – Day 1

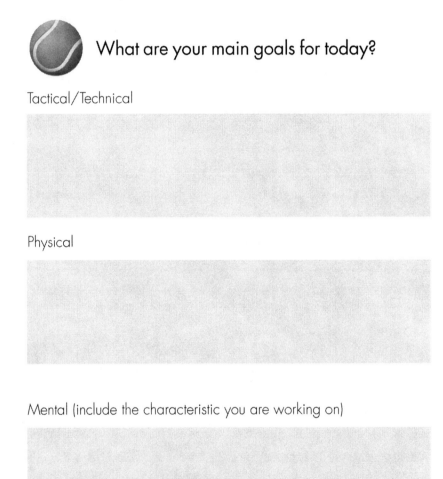

What are your main goals for today?

Tactical/Technical

Physical

Mental (include the characteristic you are working on)

How motivated were you today
(scale 1-10 where 10 is totally motivated)?

How energized were you today
(scale 1-10 where 10 is totally energized)?

List the improvements you made today?

What was one thing that you learned today that will help you in the future?

Spend 5 minutes quietly reflecting on what you did really well, no matter how small and insignificant you think it is, and feel a sense of pride throughout your whole body.

Week 1 – Day 2

 What are your main goals for today?

Tactical/Technical

Physical

Mental (include the characteristic you are working on)

How focused were you today
(scale of 1-10 where 10 is totally focused)?

How positive were you feeling today
(scale of 1-10 where 10 is totally positive)?

Did you achieve what you wanted to today? If not, what stopped you?
If yes, what was the key to your success?

What will you do to make sure you are really successful in your training
tomorrow?

Spend 5 minutes quietly reflecting on your day and committing to
yourself to make any changes you want to make tomorrow to improve
your performance.

Week 1 – Day 3

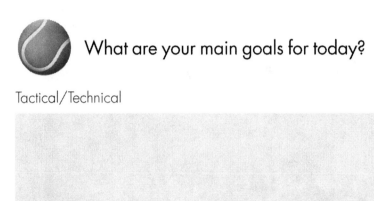 What are your main goals for today?

Tactical/Technical

Physical

Mental (include the characteristic you are working on)

How do you know you were really successful today?

List at least 3 things you did really well at today, no matter how small!

Is there anything you would like to do better at next time and if so how will you do it?

Reflect on how you lived up to your self-labels today. Be gentle on yourself if you feel you didn't achieve what you wanted and agree how you will do better tomorrow.

Week 1 – Day 4

 What are your main goals for today?

Tactical/Technical

Physical

Mental (include the characteristic you are working on)

What are all the things you did that you are most pleased with today?

What have you done today that helps you to feel more confident about your ability to perform?

Identify one situation that might happen in a match that would cause you a problem and say how you will deal with it if it happens?

Week 1 – Day 5

 What are your main goals for today?

Tactical/Technical

Physical

Mental (include the characteristic you are working on)

What challenged you most today?

What did you do to overcome those challenges? (if nothing challenged you then you need to look at the intensity of your training)

Identify one situation that might happen in a match that would cause you a problem and say how you will deal with it if it happens?

Week 1 – Day 6

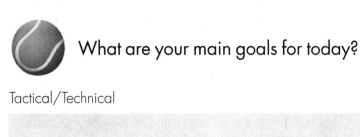 **What are your main goals for today?**

Tactical/Technical

Physical

Mental (include the characteristic you are working on)

How disciplined were you in your training today (scale 1-10 where 10 is totally disciplined)?

How much effort did you put in to training today (scale 1-10 where 10 is 100% effort)?

How do you feel about your training week? If you are pleased, what specifically are you pleased about and how will you carry this forward into next week? If you are not happy, what are you not happy about and what will you do about it for next week?

What are the things you have become aware of, about yourself and/or your performance?

Week 1 – Rest Days (1 or 2 days)

What are you going to do today to relax from tennis?

How much did you enjoy your rest day activities
(scale of 1-10 where 10 is totally enjoyed myself)?

Is there anything you would like to do more of when you are away
from tennis?

Is there anything that stops you from relaxing when away from tennis?

What did you do today that has enabled you to feel more confident
in your abilities to cope with situations outside of tennis?

Week 2 – Day 1

 What are your main goals for today?

Tactical/Technical

Physical

Mental (include the characteristic you are working on)

How motivated were you today
(scale 1-10 where 10 is totally motivated)?

How energized were you today
(scale 1-10 where 10 is totally energized)?

List the improvements you made today?

What was one thing that you learned today that will help you in the future?

Spend 5 minutes quietly reflecting on what you did really well, no matter how small and insignificant you think it is, and feel a sense of pride throughout your whole body.

Week 2 – Day 2

What are your main goals for today?

Tactical/Technical

Physical

Mental (include the characteristic you are working on)

How focused were you today
(scale of 1-10 where 10 is totally focused)?

How positive were you feeling today
(scale of 1-10 where 10 is totally positive)?

Did you achieve what you wanted to today? If not, what stopped you?
If yes, what was the key to your success?

What will you do to make sure you are really successful in your training
tomorrow?

Spend 5 minutes quietly reflecting on your day and committing to
yourself to make any changes you want to make tomorrow to improve
your performance.

Week 2 – Day 3

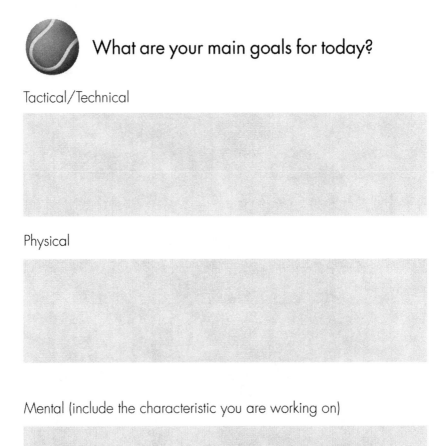

What are your main goals for today?

Tactical/Technical

Physical

Mental (include the characteristic you are working on)

How do you know you were really successful today?

List at least 3 things you did really well at today, no matter how small!

Is there anything you would like to do better at next time and if so how will you do it?

Reflect on how you lived up to your self-labels today. Be gentle on yourself if you feel you didn't achieve what you wanted and agree how you will do better tomorrow.

Week 2 – Day 4

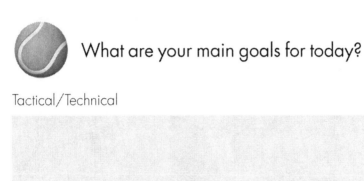 What are your main goals for today?

Tactical/Technical

Physical

Mental (include the characteristic you are working on)

What are all the things you are most pleased with today?

What have you done today that helps you to feel more confident about your ability to perform?

Identify one situation that might happen in a match that would cause you a problem and say how you will deal with it if it happens?

Week 2 – Day 5

 What are your main goals for today?

Tactical/Technical

Physical

Mental (include the characteristic you are working on)

What challenged you most today?

What did you do to overcome those challenges? (if nothing challenged you then you need to look at the intensity of your training)

Identify one situation that might happen in a match that would cause you a problem and say how you will deal with it if it happens?

Week 2 – Day 6

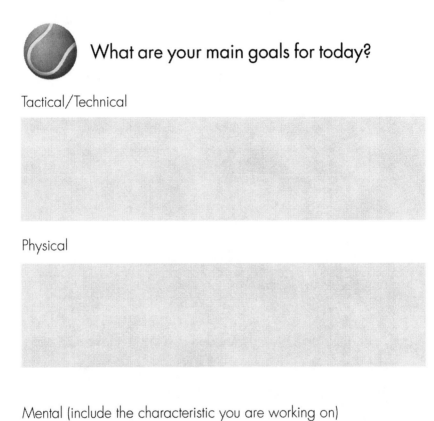 **What are your main goals for today?**

Tactical/Technical

Physical

Mental (include the characteristic you are working on)

How disciplined were you in your training today (scale 1-10 where 10 is totally disciplined)?

How much effort did you put in to training today (scale 1-10 where 10 is 100% effort)?

How do you feel about your training week? If you are pleased, what specifically are you pleased about and how will you carry this forward into next week? If you are not happy, what are you not happy about and what will you do about it for next week?

What are the things you have become aware of, about yourself and/or your performance?

Week 2 – Rest Days (1 or 2 days)

What are you going to do today to relax from tennis?

How much did you enjoy your rest day activities
(scale of 1-10 where 10 is totally enjoyed myself)?

Is there anything you would like to do more of when you are away
from tennis?

Is there anything that stops you from relaxing when away from tennis?

What did you do today that has enabled you to feel more confident
in your abilities to cope with situations outside of tennis?

Week 3 – Day 1

What are your main goals for today?

Tactical/Technical

Physical

Mental (include the characteristic you are working on)

How motivated were you today
(scale 1-10 where 10 is totally motivated)?

How energized were you today
(scale 1-10 where 10 is totally energized)?

List the improvements you made today?

What was one thing that you learned today that will help you in the future?

Spend 5 minutes quietly reflecting on what you did really well, no matter how small and insignificant you think it is, and feel a sense of pride throughout your whole body.

Week 3 – Day 2

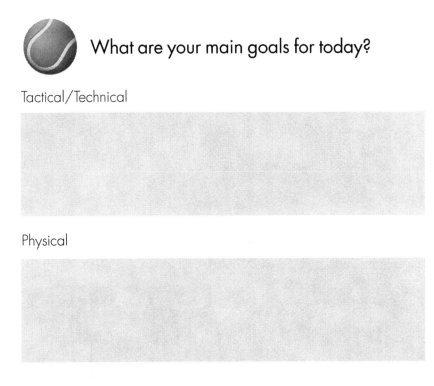 What are your main goals for today?

Tactical/Technical

Physical

Mental (include the characteristic you are working on)

How focused were you today
(scale of 1-10 where 10 is totally focused)?

How positive were you feeling today
(scale of 1-10 where 10 is totally positive)?

Did you achieve what you wanted to today? If not, what stopped you?
If yes, what was the key to your success?

What will you do to make sure you are really successful in your training
tomorrow?

Spend 5 minutes quietly reflecting on your day and committing to
yourself to make any changes you want to make tomorrow to improve
your performance.

Week 3 – Day 3

 What are your main goals for today?

Tactical/Technical

Physical

Mental (include the characteristic you are working on)

How do you know you were really successful today?

List at least 3 things you did really well at today, no matter how small!

Is there anything you would like to do better at next time and if so how will you do it?

Reflect on how you lived up to your self-labels today. Be gentle on yourself if you feel you didn't achieve what you wanted and agree how you will do better tomorrow.

Week 3 – Day 4

 What are your main goals for today?

Tactical/Technical

Physical

Mental (include the characteristic you are working on)

What are all the things you are most pleased with today?

What have you done today that helps you to feel more confident about your ability to perform?

Identify one situation that might happen in a match that would cause you a problem and say how you will deal with it if it happens?

Week 3 – Day 5

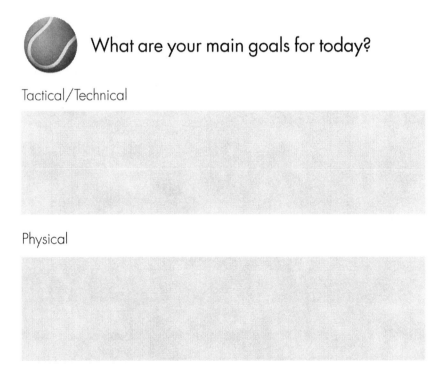

What are your main goals for today?

Tactical/Technical

Physical

Mental (include the characteristic you are working on)

What challenged you most today?

What did you do to overcome those challenges? (if nothing challenged you then you need to look at the intensity of your training)

Identify one situation that might happen in a match that would cause you a problem and say how you will deal with it if it happens?

Week 3 – Day 6

 What are your main goals for today?

Tactical/Technical

Physical

Mental (include the characteristic you are working on)

How disciplined were you in your training today (scale 1-10 where 10 is totally disciplined)?

How much effort did you put in to training today (scale 1-10 where 10 is 100% effort)?

How do you feel about your training week? If you are pleased, what specifically are you pleased about and how will you carry this forward into next week? If you are not happy, what are you not happy about and what will you do about it for next week?

What are the things you have become aware of, about yourself and/or your performance?

Week 3 – Rest Days (1 or 2 days)

What are you going to do today to relax from tennis?

How much did you enjoy your rest day activities
(scale of 1-10 where 10 is totally enjoyed myself)?

Is there anything you would like to do more of when you are away
from tennis?

Is there anything that stops you from relaxing when away from tennis?

What did you do today that has enabled you to feel more confident
in your abilities to cope with situations outside of tennis?

Week 4 – Day 1

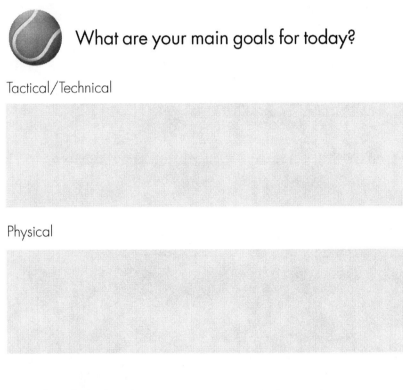 **What are your main goals for today?**

Tactical/Technical

Physical

Mental (include the characteristic you are working on)

How motivated were you today
(scale 1-10 where 10 is totally motivated)?

How energized were you today
(scale 1-10 where 10 is totally energized)?

List the improvements you made today?

What was one thing that you learned today that will help you in the future?

Spend 5 minutes quietly reflecting on what you did really well, no matter how small and insignificant you think it is, and feel a sense of pride throughout your whole body.

Week 4 – Day 2

 What are your main goals for today?

Tactical/Technical

Physical

Mental (include the characteristic you are working on)

How focused were you today
(scale of 1-10 where 10 is totally focused)?

How positive were you feeling today
(scale of 1-10 where 10 is totally positive)?

Did you achieve what you wanted to today? If not, what stopped you?
If yes, what was the key to your success?

What will you do to make sure you are really successful in your training
tomorrow?

Spend 5 minutes quietly reflecting on your day and committing to
yourself to make any changes you want to make tomorrow to improve
your performance.

Week 4 – Day 3

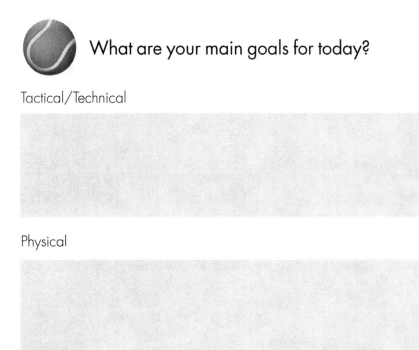 What are your main goals for today?

Tactical/Technical

Physical

Mental (include the characteristic you are working on)

How do you know you were really successful today?

List at least 3 things you did really well at today, no matter how small!

Is there anything you would like to do better at next time and if so how will you do it?

Reflect on how you lived up to your self-labels today. Be gentle on yourself if you feel you didn't achieve what you wanted and agree how you will do better tomorrow.

Week 4 – Day 4

 What are your main goals for today?

Tactical/Technical

Physical

Mental (include the characteristic you are working on)

What are all the things you are most pleased with today?

What have you done today that helps you to feel more confident about your ability to perform?

Identify one situation that might happen in a match that would cause you a problem and say how you will deal with it if it happens?

Week 4 – Day 5

 What are your main goals for today?

Tactical/Technical

Physical

Mental (include the characteristic you are working on)

What challenged you most today?

What did you do to overcome those challenges? (if nothing challenged you then you need to look at the intensity of your training)

Identify one situation that might happen in a match that would cause you a problem and say how you will deal with it if it happens?

Week 4 – Day 6

 What are your main goals for today?

Tactical/Technical

Physical

Mental (include the characteristic you are working on)

How disciplined were you in your training today (scale 1-10 where 10 is totally disciplined)?

How much effort did you put in to training today (scale 1-10 where 10 is 100% effort)?

How do you feel about your training week? If you are pleased, what specifically are you pleased about and how will you carry this forward into next week? If you are not happy, what are you not happy about and what will you do about it for next week?

What are the things you have become aware of, about yourself and/or your performance?

Week 4 – Rest Days (1 or 2 days)

What are you going to do today to relax from tennis?

How much did you enjoy your rest day activities
(scale of 1-10 where 10 is totally enjoyed myself)?

Is there anything you would like to do more of when you are away
from tennis?

Is there anything that stops you from relaxing when away from tennis?

What did you do today that has enabled you to feel more confident
in your abilities to cope with situations outside of tennis?

Training Block 1 – Review

Spend a few minutes reflecting on the last 4 weeks' training and identify at least 3 things you have improved on.

1.

2.

3.

Was there anything you didn't achieve that you wanted to achieve and if so what will you do to make sure you achieve it in the next 4 weeks?

How did the following affect your achievements...

Your motivation?

Your effort?

Your discipline?

Your focus?

Your energy?

How well did you develop your problem solving skills (SIMS)?

How much more confident are you feeling and why?

Training Block 1 – Additional Support

Did you work at developing your performance mind-set:

The quiet mind?
No evaluation?
Not trying to be perfect?
Not trying too hard, especially when things aren't going your way?
Learning to trust yourself?

Pick one aspect of the performance mind-set at a time and give your attention to it in the following 4 weeks. Be patient with yourself to develop this set of skills as they are a tough challenge.

Make sure you are looking for patterns in your behaviors and thoughts. For example, do you always lack energy after 3 days of training? Are you more motivated after a day off? Do you train with a better focus when you feel more energized? What outside influences, such as parents, school, friends or other 'stresses' affect your training? Work out what you can do about these things and add them to your goals? For example, if you feel less energized you need to warm up more vigorously. If you are less focused you need to be more disciplined with your attention. If you are not motivated you need to set some achievable goals and give 100% effort to feel good.

What achievement are you most proud of in this training block?

What did you learn about how to train more effectively?

TOP TIPS

There is a big difference between thinking and doing. Sometimes performers get stuck in thinking about what they need to do rather than doing what they need to do. They can be stuck thinking about their plan rather than delivering it.

When you take action you find the reasons to believe in yourself and what you are doing, which gives you a massive boost of confidence. Help yourself now by...

Change requires action... not just thought!

- Planning what you are going to do and sticking to it.
- Make learning about how to play the game more of a priority to you than winning.
- Over-ride any anxiety by doing the thing that is going to develop your skills and recognise that every time you overcome anxiety you are becoming mentally stronger.
- Learn to trust yourself by "just doing it" rather than worrying about what might go wrong if you do it.
- Stay focused by keeping your mind on what you want.
- Remember learning is positive and will lead you to greater success, even when you lose the match!

To get ahead in the game, you need to think in a way that enables you to succeed and also take positive action.

Training Block 2

Tactical Or Performance Goals

What are your main tactical or performance goals and specific outcomes or targets that you want to achieve in the next 4 weeks?

e.g. To remain in a neutral position after receiving a high ball to my backhand by sending the ball back deep to their backhand (assuming the backhand is the weakness).

1

2

3

4

5

Goals & Outcome Targets

Now for each of the Tactical/Performance Goals you have identified on the previous page, list the Goals/Outcome Targets that you need to achieve to improve your performance.

e.g. To ensure that I pick up the high ball early and move to take the ball at shoulder height. My outcome target is to take the ball at shoulder height 8/10 times and get the ball back cross court keeping the player behind the baseline.

1

2

3

4

5

Process Goals

What have you identified that you need to do in order to achieve your tactical/performance goals for the next 4 weeks? Include your measures of success.

MENTAL – e.g. I am going to stay focused on the opponent's racket path and ball trajectory so that I pick up the ball height as quickly as possible.

PHYSICAL – e.g. I am going to recover appropriately and then get behind every high ball so that I am in a position to take the ball below my shoulder.

TECHNICAL – e.g. I am going to ensure my swing path keeps an effective shape on the ball to get the ball back deep to the opponent, accelerating through the shot

General

How motivated are you to achieve these goals in the next 4 weeks? If you are not motivated what needs to happen for you to feel motivated?

How confident do you feel that you know what you need to achieve (process goals) in the next 4 weeks? If not what action will you take to find out what you need to achieve?

Is there anything you can think of that would stop you achieving your goals? What are you going to do to overcome any potential obstacles?

What one thing can you do to increase your chances of success in the next 4 weeks?

How can you positively label yourself? What one characteristic are you going to bring to your performance every time? e.g. smart, fighter, warrior, courageous, focused, athletic, creative... What behaviors will you adopt to achieve this characteristic? Be sure to make this characteristic a mental goal for each day!

Week 5 – Day 1

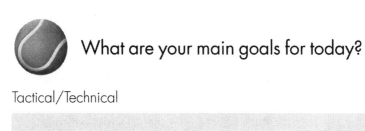 What are your main goals for today?

Tactical/Technical

Physical

Mental (include the characteristic you are working on)

How motivated were you today
(scale 1-10 where 10 is totally motivated)?

How energized were you today
(scale 1-10 where 10 is totally energized)?

List the improvements you made today?

What was one thing that you learned today that will help you in the future?

Spend 5 minutes quietly reflecting on what you did really well, no matter how small and insignificant you think it is, and feel a sense of pride throughout your whole body.

Week 5 – Day 2

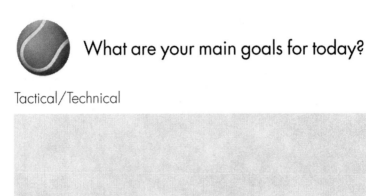 **What are your main goals for today?**

Tactical/Technical

Physical

Mental (include the characteristic you are working on)

How focused were you today
(scale of 1-10 where 10 is totally focused)?

How positive were you feeling today
(scale of 1-10 where 10 is totally positive)?

Did you achieve what you wanted to today? If not, what stopped you?
If yes, what was the key to your success?

What will you do to make sure you are really successful in your training
tomorrow?

Spend 5 minutes quietly reflecting on your day and committing to
yourself to make any changes you want to make tomorrow to improve
your performance.

Week 5 – Day 3

 What are your main goals for today?

Tactical/Technical

Physical

Mental (include the characteristic you are working on)

How do you know you were really successful today?

List at least 3 things you did really well at today, no matter how small!

Is there anything you would like to do better at next time and if so how will you do it?

Reflect on how you lived up to your self-labels today. Be gentle on yourself if you feel you didn't achieve what you wanted and agree how you will do better tomorrow.

Week 5 – Day 4

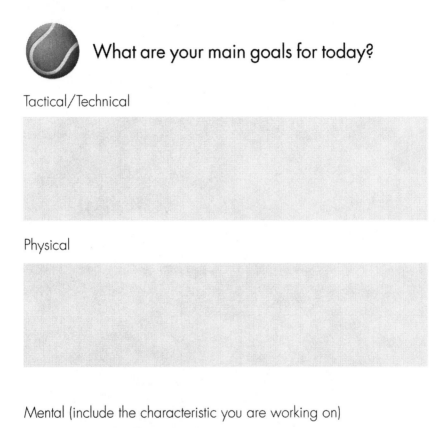

What are your main goals for today?

Tactical/Technical

Physical

Mental (include the characteristic you are working on)

What are all the things you did that you are most pleased with today?

What have you done today that helps you to feel more confident about your ability to perform?

Identify one situation that might happen in a match that would cause you a problem and say how you will deal with it if it happens?

Week 5 – Day 5

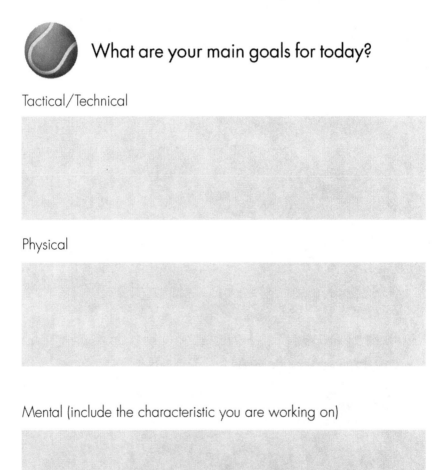

What are your main goals for today?

Tactical/Technical

Physical

Mental (include the characteristic you are working on)

What challenged you most today?

What did you do to overcome those challenges? (if nothing challenged you then you need to look at the intensity of your training)

Identify one situation that might happen in a match that would cause you a problem and say how you will deal with it if it happens?

Week 5 – Day 6

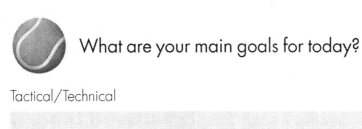 What are your main goals for today?

Tactical/Technical

Physical

Mental (include the characteristic you are working on)

How disciplined were you in your training today
(scale 1-10 where 10 is totally disciplined)?

How much effort did you put in to training today
(scale 1-10 where 10 is 100% effort)?

How do you feel about your training week? If you are pleased, what
specifically are you pleased about and how will you carry this forward
into next week? If you are not happy, what are you not happy about
and what will you do about it for next week?

What are the things you have become aware of, about yourself
and/or your performance?

Week 5 – Rest Days (1 or 2 days)

What are you going to do today to relax from tennis?

How much did you enjoy your rest day activities
(scale of 1-10 where 10 is totally enjoyed myself)?

Is there anything you would like to do more of when you are away
from tennis?

Is there anything that stops you from relaxing when away from tennis?

What did you do today that has enabled you to feel more confident
in your abilities to cope with situations outside of tennis?

Week 6 – Day 1

 What are your main goals for today?

Tactical/Technical

Physical

Mental (include the characteristic you are working on)

How motivated were you today
(scale 1-10 where 10 is totally motivated)?

How energized were you today
(scale 1-10 where 10 is totally energized)?

List the improvements you made today?

What was one thing that you learned today that will help you in the future?

Spend 5 minutes quietly reflecting on what you did really well, no matter how small and insignificant you think it is, and feel a sense of pride throughout your whole body.

Week 6 – Day 2

 What are your main goals for today?

Tactical/Technical

Physical

Mental (include the characteristic you are working on)

How focused were you today
(scale of 1-10 where 10 is totally focused)?

How positive were you feeling today
(scale of 1-10 where 10 is totally positive)?

Did you achieve what you wanted to today? If not, what stopped you?
If yes, what was the key to your success?

What will you do to make sure you are really successful in your training
tomorrow?

Spend 5 minutes quietly reflecting on your day and committing to
yourself to make any changes you want to make tomorrow to improve
your performance.

Week 6 – Day 3

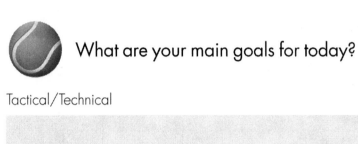 What are your main goals for today?

Tactical/Technical

Physical

Mental (include the characteristic you are working on)

How do you know you were really successful today?

List at least 3 things you did really well at today, no matter how small!

Is there anything you would like to do better at next time and if so how will you do it?

Reflect on how you lived up to your self-labels today. Be gentle on yourself if you feel you didn't achieve what you wanted and agree how you will do better tomorrow.

Week 6 – Day 4

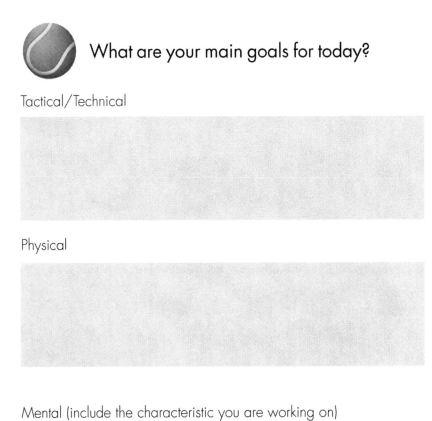 **What are your main goals for today?**

Tactical/Technical

Physical

Mental (include the characteristic you are working on)

What are all the things you are most pleased with today?

What have you done today that helps you to feel more confident about your ability to perform?

Identify one situation that might happen in a match that would cause you a problem and say how you will deal with it if it happens?

199

Week 6 – Day 5

 What are your main goals for today?

Tactical/Technical

Physical

Mental (include the characteristic you are working on)

What challenged you most today?

What did you do to overcome those challenges? (if nothing challenged you then you need to look at the intensity of your training)

Identify one situation that might happen in a match that would cause you a problem and say how you will deal with it if it happens?

Week 6 – Day 6

 What are your main goals for today?

Tactical/Technical

Physical

Mental (include the characteristic you are working on)

How disciplined were you in your training today (scale 1-10 where 10 is totally disciplined)?

How much effort did you put in to training today (scale 1-10 where 10 is 100% effort)?

How do you feel about your training week? If you are pleased, what specifically are you pleased about and how will you carry this forward into next week? If you are not happy, what are you not happy about and what will you do about it for next week?

What are the things you have become aware of, about yourself and/or your performance?

Week 6 – Rest Days (1 or 2 days)

What are you going to do today to relax from tennis?

How much did you enjoy your rest day activities
(scale of 1-10 where 10 is totally enjoyed myself)?

Is there anything you would like to do more of when you are away
from tennis?

Is there anything that stops you from relaxing when away from tennis?

What did you do today that has enabled you to feel more confident
in your abilities to cope with situations outside of tennis?

Week 7 – Day 1

 What are your main goals for today?

Tactical/Technical

Physical

Mental (include the characteristic you are working on)

How motivated were you today
(scale 1-10 where 10 is totally motivated)?

How energized were you today
(scale 1-10 where 10 is totally energized)?

List the improvements you made today?

What was one thing that you learned today that will help you in the future?

Spend 5 minutes quietly reflecting on what you did really well, no matter how small and insignificant you think it is, and feel a sense of pride throughout your whole body.

Week 7 – Day 2

 **What are your main goals for today?**

Tactical/Technical

Physical

Mental (include the characteristic you are working on)

How focused were you today
(scale of 1-10 where 10 is totally focused)?

How positive were you feeling today
(scale of 1-10 where 10 is totally positive)?

Did you achieve what you wanted to today? If not, what stopped you?
If yes, what was the key to your success?

What will you do to make sure you are really successful in your training tomorrow?

Spend 5 minutes quietly reflecting on your day and committing to yourself to make any changes you want to make tomorrow to improve your performance.

Week 7 – Day 3

 **What are your main goals for today?**

Tactical/Technical

Physical

Mental (include the characteristic you are working on)

How do you know you were really successful today?

List at least 3 things you did really well at today, no matter how small!

Is there anything you would like to do better at next time and if so how will you do it?

Reflect on how you lived up to your self-labels today. Be gentle on yourself if you feel you didn't achieve what you wanted and agree how you will do better tomorrow.

Week 7 – Day 4

 What are your main goals for today?

Tactical/Technical

Physical

Mental (include the characteristic you are working on)

What are all the things you are most pleased with today?

What have you done today that helps you to feel more confident about your ability to perform?

Identify one situation that might happen in a match that would cause you a problem and say how you will deal with it if it happens?

Week 7 – Day 5

 What are your main goals for today?

Tactical/Technical

Physical

Mental (include the characteristic you are working on)

What challenged you most today?

What did you do to overcome those challenges? (if nothing challenged you then you need to look at the intensity of your training)

Identify one situation that might happen in a match that would cause you a problem and say how you will deal with it if it happens?

Week 7 – Day 6

What are your main goals for today?

Tactical/Technical

Physical

Mental (include the characteristic you are working on)

How disciplined were you in your training today
(scale 1-10 where 10 is totally disciplined)?

How much effort did you put in to training today
(scale 1-10 where 10 is 100% effort)?

How do you feel about your training week? If you are pleased, what
specifically are you pleased about and how will you carry this forward
into next week? If you are not happy, what are you not happy about
and what will you do about it for next week?

What are the things you have become aware of, about yourself
and/or your performance?

Week 7 – Rest Days (1 or 2 days)

What are you going to do today to relax from tennis?

How much did you enjoy your rest day activities
(scale of 1-10 where 10 is totally enjoyed myself)?

Is there anything you would like to do more of when you are away
from tennis?

Is there anything that stops you from relaxing when away from tennis?

What did you do today that has enabled you to feel more confident
in your abilities to cope with situations outside of tennis?

Week 8 – Day 1

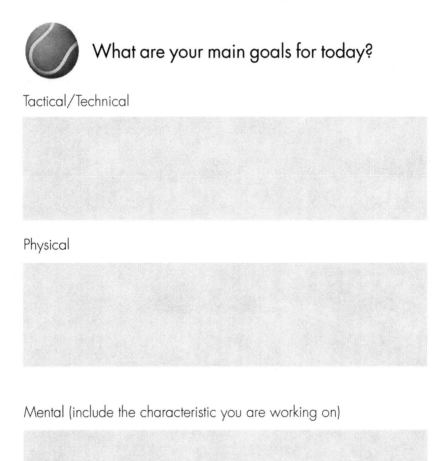

What are your main goals for today?

Tactical/Technical

Physical

Mental (include the characteristic you are working on)

How motivated were you today
(scale 1-10 where 10 is totally motivated)?

How energized were you today
(scale 1-10 where 10 is totally energized)?

List the improvements you made today?

What was one thing that you learned today that will help you in the future?

Spend 5 minutes quietly reflecting on what you did really well, no matter how small and insignificant you think it is, and feel a sense of pride throughout your whole body.

Week 8 – Day 2

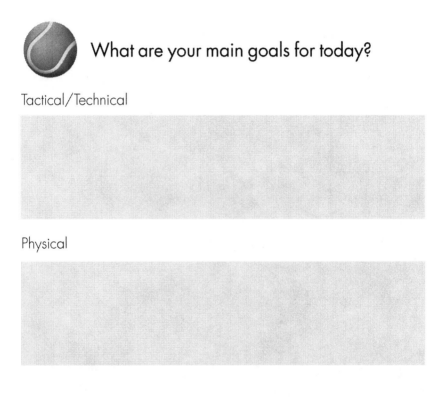 **What are your main goals for today?**

Tactical/Technical

Physical

Mental (include the characteristic you are working on)

How focused were you today
(scale of 1-10 where 10 is totally focused)?

How positive were you feeling today
(scale of 1-10 where 10 is totally positive)?

Did you achieve what you wanted to today? If not, what stopped you?
If yes, what was the key to your success?

What will you do to make sure you are really successful in your training
tomorrow?

Spend 5 minutes quietly reflecting on your day and committing to
yourself to make any changes you want to make tomorrow to improve
your performance.

Week 8 – Day 3

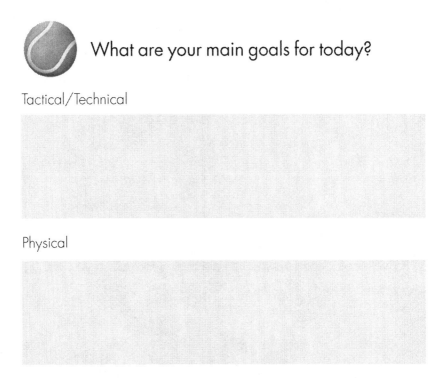 What are your main goals for today?

Tactical/Technical

Physical

Mental (include the characteristic you are working on)

How do you know you were really successful today?

List at least 3 things you did really well at today, no matter how small!

Is there anything you would like to do better at next time and if so how will you do it?

Reflect on how you lived up to your self-labels today. Be gentle on yourself if you feel you didn't achieve what you wanted and agree how you will do better tomorrow.

225

Week 8 – Day 4

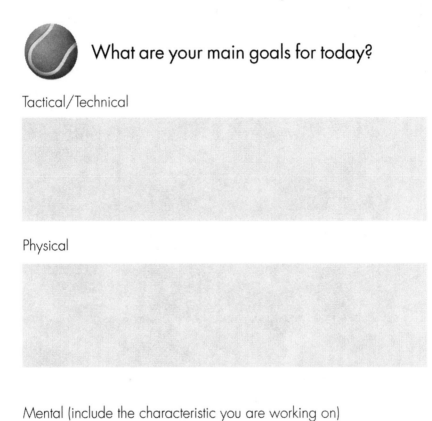 What are your main goals for today?

Tactical/Technical

Physical

Mental (include the characteristic you are working on)

What are all the things you are most pleased with today?

What have you done today that helps you to feel more confident about your ability to perform?

Identify one situation that might happen in a match that would cause you a problem and say how you will deal with it if it happens?

Week 8 – Day 5

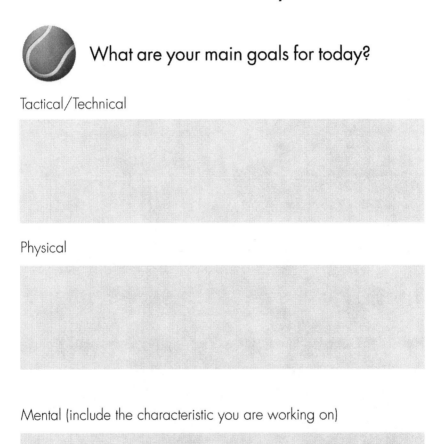 **What are your main goals for today?**

Tactical/Technical

Physical

Mental (include the characteristic you are working on)

What challenged you most today?

What did you do to overcome those challenges? (if nothing challenged you then you need to look at the intensity of your training)

Identify one situation that might happen in a match that would cause you a problem and say how you will deal with it if it happens?

Week 8 – Day 6

 What are your main goals for today?

Tactical/Technical

Physical

Mental (include the characteristic you are working on)

How disciplined were you in your training today (scale 1-10 where 10 is totally disciplined)?

How much effort did you put in to training today (scale 1-10 where 10 is 100% effort)?

How do you feel about your training week? If you are pleased, what specifically are you pleased about and how will you carry this forward into next week? If you are not happy, what are you not happy about and what will you do about it for next week?

What are the things you have become aware of, about yourself and/or your performance?

Week 1 – Rest Days (1 or 2 days)

What are you going to do today to relax from tennis?

How much did you enjoy your rest day activities
(scale of 1-10 where 10 is totally enjoyed myself)?

Is there anything you would like to do more of when you are away
from tennis?

Is there anything that stops you from relaxing when away from tennis?

What did you do today that has enabled you to feel more confident
in your abilities to cope with situations outside of tennis?

Training Block 2 – Review

Spend a few minutes reflecting on the last 4 weeks training and identify at least 3 things you have improved on.

1.

2.

3.

Was there anything you didn't achieve that you wanted to achieve and if so what will you do to make sure you achieve it in the next block?

How well did you develop your positive self-labels?

How disciplined have you been in continuing the work you are doing on a one-to-one with your coach, in the squad situation?

What have you done that has helped you to feel more confident during the last 4 weeks?

Training Block 2 – Additional Support

To what extent are you motivated by the outcomes rather than by the effort you put into your training? You need to learn to value the effort you put in, even if you don't get immediate results.

When reviewing your training day, become aware of whether you have been mentally and emotionally engaged in what you have been doing as this will affect your focus of attention. Were you distracted and if so by what?

Remember that whatever you train you perfect, including your attitude. The work you do with an individual coach will take longer to transform into your performances if you forget it all when playing in squads or training matches.

One of the most important skills you can develop is that of self-honesty. You are human and as such you are not perfect and you will not remember to do everything that is asked of you in training. Be honest about what you put into your tennis and become aware of when this changes. There will be a relationship between what you put in mentally and the outcomes you get (physically and technically) and a big part of your development is to find out what that relationship is so that you can put in the best ingredients to get the outcomes you want.

Pay particular attention to your mood states, your self-talk, your attitude, your diet, your energy levels and any shifts in hormones. These will all affect your results in training and in matches.

TOP TIPS

How you measure your success will determine how you feel about what you are doing. You need to learn to measure your progress so that you realize you are improving. You may also need to maintain your skills so it isn't always about bigger numbers! Help yourself now by...

What you measure determines how you feel about what you are doing

- Think of yourself as banking what you do. Whatever you achieve in training is being stored for you to call on at a later date. You may not get a return on your investment immediately, but with time and greater investments your efforts are sure to pay off.
- Look for the things you have done well, no matter how small and recognise that lots of small things improving leads to a massive improvement over time.
- Make sure you are measuring what you can control and not undermining your confidence by focusing on what you cannot control.
- Remember that improvement isn't a simple linear process of improving every day. Think of it this way... you are trying to raise your averages, not be perfect. By increasing your average performance and making the difference between your best and worst performances small, you will become a consistently solid performer.

Training Block 3

Tactical Or Performance Goals

What are your main tactical or performance goals and specific outcomes or targets that you want to achieve in the next 4 weeks?

e.g. To develop my first serve out wide to pressurise their backhand return, to enable me to take control of the point early.

1

2

3

4

5

Goals & Outcome Targets

Now for each of the Tactical/Performance Goals you have identified on the previous page, list the Goals/Outcome Targets that you need to achieve to improve your performance.

e.g. To hit serve wide to the backhand pulling the player outside the tramlines making it tough for them to return. My outcome target for this is to hit the effective wide serve 7/10 times – effective means that their return puts me in an attacking position.

1

2

3

4

5

Process Goals

What have you identified that you need to do in order to achieve your tactical/performance goals for the next 4 weeks? Include your measures of success.

MENTAL – e.g. I am going to be disciplined with my pre-serve routine to get a good image of where I want to serve to and take care of my ball toss so that I only hit the serve when the ball is in the right place.

PHYSICAL – e.g. I am going to be explosive into my serve using my legs to drive power into my serve.

TECHNICAL – e.g. I am going to keep a dolphin shape (or elephant's trunk) shape on my serve to ensure that I get the right shape on my service action.

General

How motivated are you to achieve these goals in the next 4 weeks? If you are not motivated what needs to happen for you to feel motivated?

How confident do you feel that you know what you need to achieve (process goals) in the next 4 weeks? If not what action will you take to find out what you need to achieve?

How confident do you feel that you know what you need to achieve (process goals) in the next 4 weeks? If not what action will you take to find out what you need to achieve?

Is there anything you can think of that would stop you achieving your goals? What are you going to do to overcome any potential obstacles?

What one thing can you do to increase your chances of success in the next 4 weeks?

How can you positively label yourself? What one characteristic are you going to bring to your performance every time? e.g. smart, fighter, warrior, courageous, focused, athletic, creative... What behaviors will you adopt to achieve this characteristic? Be sure to make this characteristic a mental goal for each day!

Week 9 – Day 1

 What are your main goals for today?

Tactical/Technical

Physical

Mental (include the characteristic you are working on)

How motivated were you today
(scale 1-10 where 10 is totally motivated)?

How energized were you today
(scale 1-10 where 10 is totally energized)?

List the improvements you made today?

What was one thing that you learned today that will help you in the future?

Spend 5 minutes quietly reflecting on what you did really well, no matter how small and insignificant you think it is, and feel a sense of pride throughout your whole body.

Week 9 – Day 2

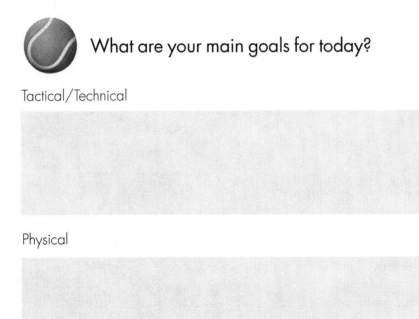 **What are your main goals for today?**

Tactical/Technical

Physical

Mental (include the characteristic you are working on)

How focused were you today
(scale of 1-10 where 10 is totally focused)?

How positive were you feeling today
(scale of 1-10 where 10 is totally positive)?

Did you achieve what you wanted to today? If not, what stopped you?
If yes, what was the key to your success?

What will you do to make sure you are really successful in your training
tomorrow?

Spend 5 minutes quietly reflecting on your day and committing to
yourself to make any changes you want to make tomorrow to improve
your performance.

Week 9 – Day 3

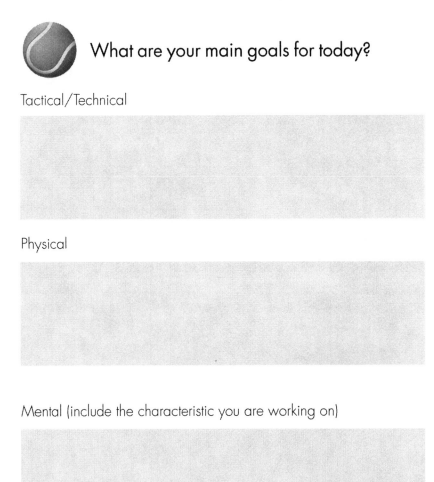 **What are your main goals for today?**

Tactical/Technical

Physical

Mental (include the characteristic you are working on)

How do you know you were really successful today?

List at least 3 things you did really well at today, no matter how small!

Is there anything you would like to do better at next time and if so how will you do it?

Reflect on how you lived up to your self-labels today. Be gentle on yourself if you feel you didn't achieve what you wanted and agree how you will do better tomorrow.

Week 9 – Day 4

 What are your main goals for today?

Tactical/Technical

Physical

Mental (include the characteristic you are working on)

What are all the things you did that you are most pleased with today?

What have you done today that helps you to feel more confident about your ability to perform?

Identify one situation that might happen in a match that would cause you a problem and say how you will deal with it if it happens?

Week 9 – Day 5

 **What are your main goals for today?**

Tactical/Technical

Physical

Mental (include the characteristic you are working on)

What challenged you most today?

What did you do to overcome those challenges? (if nothing challenged you then you need to look at the intensity of your training)

Identify one situation that might happen in a match that would cause you a problem and say how you will deal with it if it happens?

Week 9 – Day 6

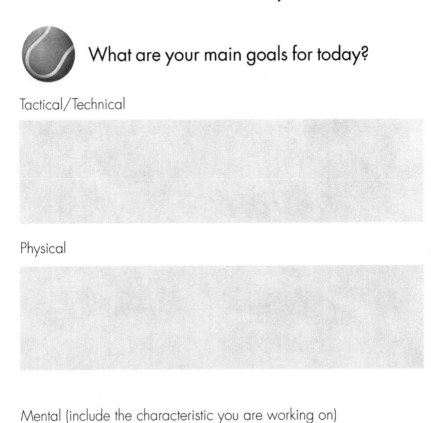

What are your main goals for today?

Tactical/Technical

Physical

Mental (include the characteristic you are working on)

How disciplined were you in your training today (scale 1-10 where 10 is totally disciplined)?

How much effort did you put in to training today (scale 1-10 where 10 is 100% effort)?

How do you feel about your training week? If you are pleased, what specifically are you pleased about and how will you carry this forward into next week? If you are not happy, what are you not happy about and what will you do about it for next week?

What are the things you have become aware of, about yourself and/or your performance?

Week 9 – Rest Days (1 or 2 days)

What are you going to do today to relax from tennis?

How much did you enjoy your rest day activities
(scale of 1-10 where 10 is totally enjoyed myself)?

Is there anything you would like to do more of when you are away
from tennis?

Is there anything that stops you from relaxing when away from tennis?

What did you do today that has enabled you to feel more confident
in your abilities to cope with situations outside of tennis?

Week 10 – Day 1

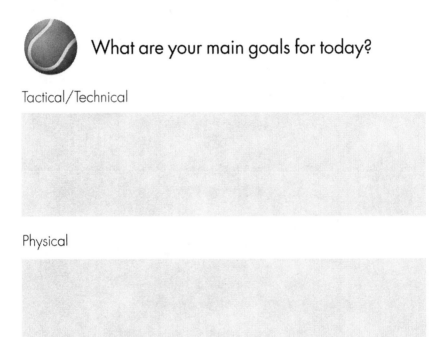 What are your main goals for today?

Tactical/Technical

Physical

Mental (include the characteristic you are working on)

How motivated were you today
(scale 1-10 where 10 is totally motivated)?

How energized were you today
(scale 1-10 where 10 is totally energized)?

List the improvements you made today?

What was one thing that you learned today that will help you in the future?

Spend 5 minutes quietly reflecting on what you did really well, no matter how small and insignificant you think it is, and feel a sense of pride throughout your whole body.

Week 10 – Day 2

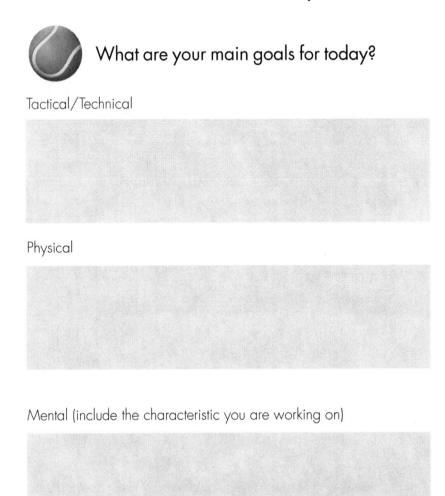

What are your main goals for today?

Tactical/Technical

Physical

Mental (include the characteristic you are working on)

How focused were you today
(scale of 1-10 where 10 is totally focused)?

How positive were you feeling today
(scale of 1-10 where 10 is totally positive)?

Did you achieve what you wanted to today? If not, what stopped you?
If yes, what was the key to your success?

What will you do to make sure you are really successful in your training
tomorrow?

Spend 5 minutes quietly reflecting on your day and committing to
yourself to make any changes you want to make tomorrow to improve
your performance.

Week 10 – Day 3

 What are your main goals for today?

Tactical/Technical

Physical

Mental (include the characteristic you are working on)

How do you know you were really successful today?

List at least 3 things you did really well at today, no matter how small!

Is there anything you would like to do better at next time and if so how will you do it?

Reflect on how you lived up to your self-labels today. Be gentle on yourself if you feel you didn't achieve what you wanted and agree how you will do better tomorrow.

Week 10 – Day 4

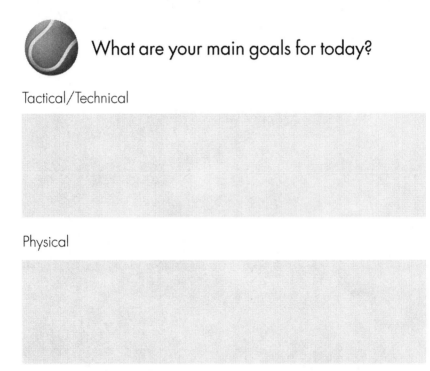 **What are your main goals for today?**

Tactical/Technical

Physical

Mental (include the characteristic you are working on)

What are all the things you are most pleased with today?

What have you done today that helps you to feel more confident about your ability to perform?

Identify one situation that might happen in a match that would cause you a problem and say how you will deal with it if it happens?

Week 10 – Day 5

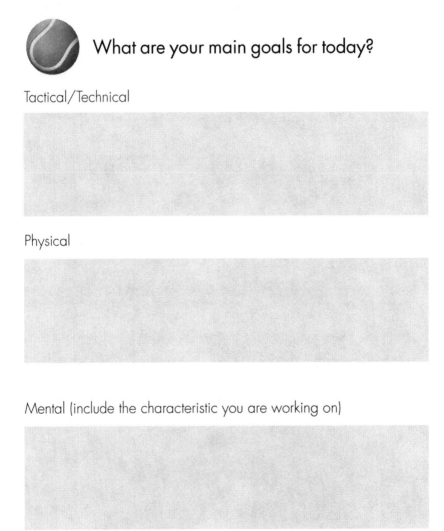 **What are your main goals for today?**

Tactical/Technical

Physical

Mental (include the characteristic you are working on)

What challenged you most today?

What did you do to overcome those challenges? (if nothing challenged you then you need to look at the intensity of your training)

Identify one situation that might happen in a match that would cause you a problem and say how you will deal with it if it happens?

Week 10 – Day 6

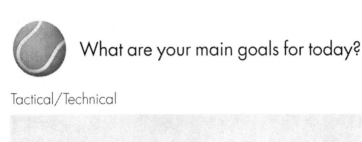 What are your main goals for today?

Tactical/Technical

Physical

Mental (include the characteristic you are working on)

How disciplined were you in your training today (scale 1-10 where 10 is totally disciplined)?

How much effort did you put in to training today (scale 1-10 where 10 is 100% effort)?

How do you feel about your training week? If you are pleased, what specifically are you pleased about and how will you carry this forward into next week? If you are not happy, what are you not happy about and what will you do about it for next week?

What are the things you have become aware of, about yourself and/or your performance?

Week 10 – Rest Days (1 or 2 days)

What are you going to do today to relax from tennis?

How much did you enjoy your rest day activities
(scale of 1-10 where 10 is totally enjoyed myself)?

Is there anything you would like to do more of when you are away
from tennis?

Is there anything that stops you from relaxing when away from tennis?

What did you do today that has enabled you to feel more confident
in your abilities to cope with situations outside of tennis?

Week 11 – Day 1

 What are your main goals for today?

Tactical/Technical

Physical

Mental (include the characteristic you are working on)

How motivated were you today
(scale 1-10 where 10 is totally motivated)?

How energized were you today
(scale 1-10 where 10 is totally energized)?

List the improvements you made today?

What was one thing that you learned today that will help you in the future?

Spend 5 minutes quietly reflecting on what you did really well, no matter how small and insignificant you think it is, and feel a sense of pride throughout your whole body.

Week 11 – Day 2

 What are your main goals for today?

Tactical/Technical

Physical

Mental (include the characteristic you are working on)

How focused were you today
(scale of 1-10 where 10 is totally focused)?

How positive were you feeling today
(scale of 1-10 where 10 is totally positive)?

Did you achieve what you wanted to today? If not, what stopped you?
If yes, what was the key to your success?

What will you do to make sure you are really successful in your training
tomorrow?

Spend 5 minutes quietly reflecting on your day and committing to
yourself to make any changes you want to make tomorrow to improve
your performance.

Week 11 – Day 3

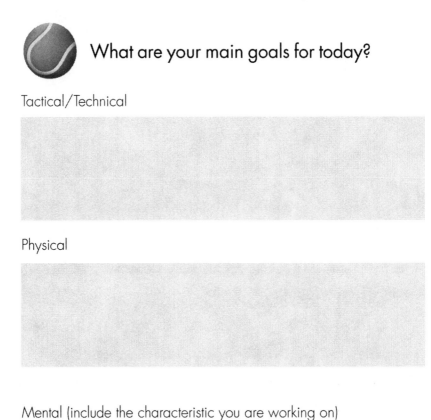 What are your main goals for today?

Tactical/Technical

Physical

Mental (include the characteristic you are working on)

How do you know you were really successful today?

List at least 3 things you did really well at today, no matter how small!

Is there anything you would like to do better at next time and if so how will you do it?

Reflect on how you lived up to your self-labels today. Be gentle on yourself if you feel you didn't achieve what you wanted and agree how you will do better tomorrow.

Week 11 – Day 4

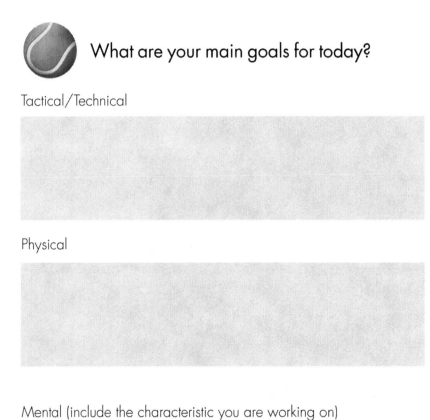 What are your main goals for today?

Tactical/Technical

Physical

Mental (include the characteristic you are working on)

What are all the things you are most pleased with today?

What have you done today that helps you to feel more confident about your ability to perform?

Identify one situation that might happen in a match that would cause you a problem and say how you will deal with it if it happens?

Week 11 – Day 5

 What are your main goals for today?

Tactical/Technical

Physical

Mental (include the characteristic you are working on)

What challenged you most today?

What did you do to overcome those challenges? (if nothing challenged you then you need to look at the intensity of your training)

Identify one situation that might happen in a match that would cause you a problem and say how you will deal with it if it happens?

Week 11 – Day 6

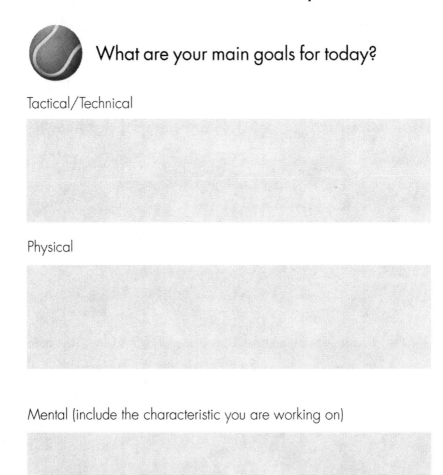 What are your main goals for today?

Tactical/Technical

Physical

Mental (include the characteristic you are working on)

How disciplined were you in your training today
(scale 1-10 where 10 is totally disciplined)?

How much effort did you put in to training today
(scale 1-10 where 10 is 100% effort)?

How do you feel about your training week? If you are pleased, what
specifically are you pleased about and how will you carry this forward
into next week? If you are not happy, what are you not happy about
and what will you do about it for next week?

What are the things you have become aware of, about yourself
and/or your performance?

Week 11 – Rest Days (1 or 2 days)

What are you going to do today to relax from tennis?

How much did you enjoy your rest day activities
(scale of 1-10 where 10 is totally enjoyed myself)?

Is there anything you would like to do more of when you are away
from tennis?

Is there anything that stops you from relaxing when away from tennis?

What did you do today that has enabled you to feel more confident
in your abilities to cope with situations outside of tennis?

Week 12 – Day 1

 What are your main goals for today?

Tactical/Technical

Physical

Mental (include the characteristic you are working on)

How motivated were you today
(scale 1-10 where 10 is totally motivated)?

How energized were you today
(scale 1-10 where 10 is totally energized)?

List the improvements you made today?

What was one thing that you learned today that will help you in the future?

Spend 5 minutes quietly reflecting on what you did really well, no matter how small and insignificant you think it is, and feel a sense of pride throughout your whole body.

Week 12 – Day 2

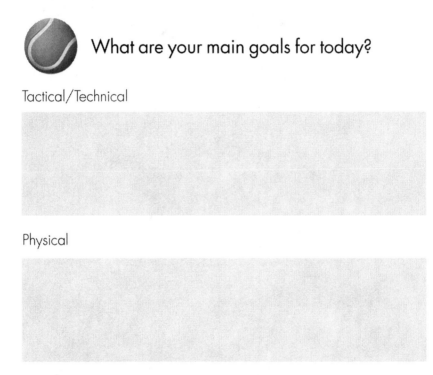 What are your main goals for today?

Tactical/Technical

Physical

Mental (include the characteristic you are working on)

How focused were you today
(scale of 1-10 where 10 is totally focused)?

How positive were you feeling today
(scale of 1-10 where 10 is totally positive)?

Did you achieve what you wanted to today? If not, what stopped you?
If yes, what was the key to your success?

What will you do to make sure you are really successful in your training
tomorrow?

Spend 5 minutes quietly reflecting on your day and committing to
yourself to make any changes you want to make tomorrow to improve
your performance.

Week 12 – Day 3

 What are your main goals for today?

Tactical/Technical

Physical

Mental (include the characteristic you are working on)

How do you know you were really successful today?

List at least 3 things you did really well at today, no matter how small!

Is there anything you would like to do better at next time and if so how will you do it?

Reflect on how you lived up to your self-labels today. Be gentle on yourself if you feel you didn't achieve what you wanted and agree how you will do better tomorrow.

Week 12 – Day 4

 What are your main goals for today?

Tactical/Technical

Physical

Mental (include the characteristic you are working on)

What are all the things you are most pleased with today?

What have you done today that helps you to feel more confident about your ability to perform?

Identify one situation that might happen in a match that would cause you a problem and say how you will deal with it if it happens?

Week 12 – Day 5

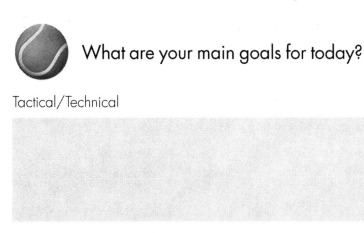 What are your main goals for today?

Tactical/Technical

Physical

Mental (include the characteristic you are working on)

What challenged you most today?

What did you do to overcome those challenges? (if nothing challenged you then you need to look at the intensity of your training)

Identify one situation that might happen in a match that would cause you a problem and say how you will deal with it if it happens?

Week 12 – Day 6

 What are your main goals for today?

Tactical/Technical

Physical

Mental (include the characteristic you are working on)

How disciplined were you in your training today (scale 1-10 where 10 is totally disciplined)?

How much effort did you put in to training today (scale 1-10 where 10 is 100% effort)?

How do you feel about your training week? If you are pleased, what specifically are you pleased about and how will you carry this forward into next week? If you are not happy, what are you not happy about and what will you do about it for next week?

What are the things you have become aware of, about yourself and/or your performance?

Week 12 – Rest Days (1 or 2 days)

What are you going to do today to relax from tennis?

How much did you enjoy your rest day activities
(scale of 1-10 where 10 is totally enjoyed myself)?

Is there anything you would like to do more of when you are away
from tennis?

Is there anything that stops you from relaxing when away from tennis?

What did you do today that has enabled you to feel more confident
in your abilities to cope with situations outside of tennis?

Training Block 3 – Review

Spend a few minutes reflecting on the last 4 weeks training and identify at least 3 things you have improved on.

Was there anything you didn't achieve that you wanted to achieve and if so what will you do to make sure you achieve it in the next block?

Does the level of intensity of your training support you in being able to handle the competitive arena? If not what can you do about it?

How much more confident are you feeling and why?

Training Block 3 – Additional Support

How honest have you been with yourself during this training block? If you have been honest you will have increasingly higher levels of self awareness. If you are not able to be honest with yourself, try to understand why this is the case and see if you can commit to honesty moving forward.

How gentle have you been with yourself? Reducing any negative self-talk and instead replacing it with objectivity and compassion will help you to value what you are doing rather than seeing yourself as an under achiever or failure.

Remember that practice is your goal, not perfection. The journey of continuous improvement means that there is no end to the improvements you can make and the opportunities that are available to you. You are never finished, you are just able to be successful at a higher level than you would have done in the past.

Make sure that your training always has a purpose. Mindless training is a waste of time. Mindful training is exciting, rewarding and builds confidence. Always make sure you know why you are doing what you are doing in training and make sure it all helps you to perform better.

Always look to understand the broader skills that are being developed in everything you do. Training is about more than hitting balls! The drills are about more than developing the technical/tactical skill, they are also about developing the physical and mental skills.

TOP TIPS

Developing a system of measurement that works for you is important because it is something that motivates and helps you to feel in control of your development. Consistency and continuous repetition are necessary for you to create positive permanent habits. Your task is never ending and your journey is one of continuous improvement. Over the last 12 weeks you will have answered a

Developing positive habits requires consistent and continuous repetition. There is no end!

number of questions to help you to create a effective process of evaluation and measurement for yourself. You will know how you have improved and if you haven't. You can continue to help yourself into the future now by…

- Identifying what is the most helpful information for you to keep a track of in respect of your training
- Ensuring you keep raising your awareness to how you achieve the results you get rather than blaming things or making excuses when things don't go your way
- Ensuring you keep tennis in perspective so that it doesn't dominate your life in an unhealthy way
- Learning to appreciate the broader skills that you are developing as you continue on your tennis journey. Tennis is a way to develop yourself and in developing yourself you will develop some personal skills that will ensure you are successful no matter what you do in life

Competing

I presume that you are training for a reason and that reason is because you love to compete. Recording, measurement and evaluation are important aspects of being a determined competitor because you can use the information you gather from your competitive performances to inform your training and development.

There are two ways to approach a competition. The first is simply with your eyes on the outcome... just wanting to win. The second is to set yourself some objectives for the match that keep you focused on what is important... what you need to do to win. Those players who just focus on wanting to win can experience a lot of problems, higher levels of anxiety, greater fluctuations in performance from excellent to rubbish, fragile confidence, high levels of doubt and may also experience things like tanking and losing interest. The player who sets themselves targets or goals for the match is most likely to learn the most, develop the fastest, feel they are achieving, build their confidence and get better and more consistent results.

In the final part of this log-book, I have presented a series of questions for you to use, so that you can understand how to effectively approach the monitoring and evaluation of your competitive performances. This will help you to learn from what you do competitively and then bring that information back into your training to work on, to improve your competitive results. You will need to be selective over the questions you answer and only work with the questions that apply to you now. That is to say, work with the questions that when you answer them will give you the best insights into your performance and how to progress. Initially you may wish to go through all the questions to see which ones are the most revealing for you. As you do this you will raise your awareness to the most important areas for you to work on.

Pre-Match Information To Collect

- Where are you playing?
- What is the surface?
- Date and time of day you are playing?
- Name of opponent and ranking/rating and/or age?
- Weather conditions?
- How you feel about playing under the conditions you have just written down?

Personal Pre-Match

(you can use a scale of 1-10 where 10 is excellent/positive)

1. How well did you sleep?
2. How well have you eaten before the match?
3. How well did you physically warm up?
4. How well did you do a tennis warm up?
5. How do you feel about playing your opponent?
6. How up for it are you feeling?
7. How focused are you feeling (on what you are going to do in the match)?
8. What are your goals/tactical outcomes for your match?
9. How strongly do you believe your plan will get you the outcome you want today? Remember, you should feel that your plan will give you the best chance of winning. There are no guarantees that you will win, even if you do execute your plan well because your opponent could play better than you!
10. If anything is distracting you what is it and what are you going to do about it to stop it being a distraction?

⓫ What cue words are you going to use to keep you on track, tactically, technically, mentally and physically?

⓬ How well do you know your between point routine?

⓭ How committed are you to achieving your goals even if the going gets tough?

⓮ What have you done to handle any nerves?

Breathing, exercising, positive self talk, know how you will handle anything that comes up, set goals to keep your mind occupied.

⓯ What have you done to help yourself to feel confident?

Reflect on: what you do well and how you can exploit your strengths, how well you train for competing, your past successes, visualise success now, commit to doing the best you can and let the result take care of itself, know how you will cope if things don't go your way, know how you will problem solve during the match, put your learning before the result

⓰ What will you do if you feel a bit rusty in the warm up?

Keep your feet moving, relax your upper body and keep your focus on the ball, hit within yourself and build up the pace and tempo rather than hitting full out from the start, have bigger margins and focus on creating the shape of shot you want. Stop any negative thoughts and stay focused on what you are going to achieve tactically. Learn as much as you can about your opponent in the warm up, but remember you are not trying to beat him/her here!

⓱ What positive label are you going to achieve in your match today?

⓲ Which aspect of the performance mind-set are you going to work at today in your match?

⓳ Have 3 very clear process measures of success before you play (winning should not be one of these measures because you do not have full control of it).

There is a great deal of information you will get from answering the questions above and it is important that you do not go into your match with too many things in your head. The questions above are there to get you thinking, so please only pick the things that are most appropriate for you. Pick the things that are going to help you stay on track during the match and get the best out of yourself. You should answer the first 7 questions above every time you perform as these are giving you information about how you started the match. From a mental perspective your performance starts from when you wake up in the morning. Your mood state, diet, warm up and attitude towards the match and your opponent will all affect how you perform and particularly how you start the match. Look for patterns in these things and link them to whether you start well or slowly. Then make sure you do what it takes to give yourself the best start possible.

As a general principle please avoid superstition as this is not helpful. Having to wear a particular item of clothing in order to play well is fine as long as you can guarantee you have the item in your bag, but having to see a black cat before you play for good luck is not going to help you! The reality is this... the more barriers you put in place that you link with your success, the harder it will be for you to achieve your highest potential in tennis. Superstition is not helpful as it too easily back fires on you. Instead work with the truth... you will get out of your performance only what you put in. Take care of the ingredients you put in to get the result you want and remember that you do not have full control over the winning or losing of the match. You do have full control over whether you choose to put in your best ingredients or not. Making the right choices is going to enhance your confidence far more than winning matches through luck and superstition.

Post-Match Evaluation

Even though you may not feel like you want to do a post-match evaluation, reviewing your successes and the points you need to learn from is a critical part of your development. Your post-match evaluation needs to be in alignment with your objectives for the match so that you stay focused on what you went into the match to achieve, rather than getting distracted by everything that happened in the match. There are some general questions and more specfic questions below that you can use below to support your post-match evaluation.

1. How do you feel about your performance and why?
2. What do you feel you did well?
3. What did you learn?
4. How well did you maintain your emotional state?
5. How well did you manage any nerves or anxiety?
6. How well did you stick to your intended goals?
7. How well did you move your feet / recover during the match?
8. How well did you problem solve when in trouble (SIMS)?
9. How well did you handle pressure – what did you do?
10. How quiet did you keep your mind?
11. How well did you refrain from judging your performance negatively?
12. How well did you avoid the temptation to try too hard?
13. How well did you avoid the tempatation to hit the ball perfectly?
14. How well did you trust yourself (rather than doubt yourself)?
15. If you doubted yourself, what happened that caused you to do this?
16. What distracted you and how can you deal with that next time? (Discipline of concentration is the cure for distraction!)

17. How well did you do your routines between points and games? (You will know you have done well if you remained in a good emotional state, stayed focused on your plan, relaxed between points and games and learned from your experience)

18. How tactically effective were you? Did you get the outcomes you were trying for? If not why not?

19. How did you win points? Tactically what did you do to the other player?

20. How were points won against you? Tactically what did they do to you?

21. How has your awareness improved? What are you aware of now that you weren't before?

22. What would you do differently if you were playing that match again tomorrow?

23. How much more confident do you feel about your performance? If not, how do you need to look at your performance differently in order to see the progress you are making? (Confidence based on winning will be fragile).

Again, there are a number of questions here and my intention is for you to choose the most appropriate questions that help you to appreciate your performance, learn to evaluate effectively and raise your awareness. Work with 2 or 3 questions for a period of time rather than trying to do too much too quickly. The most important thing to remember is to never see what you have done as failing. A simple principle to embrace is that there is no failure, only feedback. This means that your job is simply to understand in every match the ingredients that you put in that contributed to you getting the results you did. Then understand how your ingredients and your opponent's ingredients together with the external conditions influenced the outcome of the game. If you were successful, ask would you still be successful with the same ingredients at the next level? If your opponent's ingredients got a better outcome than you, ask yourself what you would have needed to do differently to get a better outcome against them?

I am sure you could think of other questions to ask yourself to understand objectively what went on in your performance. As a general principle, if you lose emotional control you will be unable to think well on the court and this will make any evaluation difficult because your results are skewed by your emotional state, which affects your brain and your body. Remember that you are looking for patterns in what you do. The good patterns you repeat and the less effective patterns you change. As a result of an effective evaluation it should become very clear to you what you need to do in your training and therefore your goals for training can be set to complete the cycle.

Conclusion

We have now come to the end of this part of your journey to help you to transform how you perform. But, this is not really the end. It is just the beginning. If you have taken a massive amount of action throughout this program you will really be feeling the benefits and seeing the transformation in your game. Please continue this process into the future and you will, without doubt, achieve your highest potential. As you know, no-one can promise you the ultimate prize of being World No 1. But, you will know that no matter what you have achieved, you have done as well as you could. Because you will be able to say that, you will also feel a great sense of confidence in yourself and your achievements. You will have developed some very significant mental skills along the way that will continue to ensure your success in life, way beyond your career in tennis. You will feel good about yourself and your achievements and you will know that it was all worth it.

If, along your journey, now or in the future, you have any questions or would like further information or advice in becoming a Peak Performer, either as a player or a coach then please do visit my website: www.academyforpeakperformance.co.uk

Achieving Peak Performance In Tennis

A practical guide to developing your mind and energy system for winning

by Helen K. Emms

Available from Amazon and
www.liveitpublishing.com

Achieving Peak Performance in Tennis gives you a comprehensive and new understanding of your mental game including psychological and energetic influences that you will not have considered before now.

Read this book and learn how to successfully overcome the instinctive drives that limit your game and how to raise your awareness to achieve your highest potential.

Bring the joy of tennis back into your game by discovering how to: Deal with pressure, perfectionism and expectations; Build self-esteem, self-belief and confidence; Develop emotional control, resilience and inner mental strength; Stop trying so hard and get better results; turn failure into success and much, much more!

Changing Mindsets & Developing Spirit

Inspirational coaching through verse
for success in sport and life

by Helen K. Emms

*Available from Amazon and
www.liveitpublishing.com*

There is a force in each of us that compels us to overcome our limitations and strive to experience ourselves and our life at its very best. Yet many of us struggle to be all that we can be. By changing our mind 'sets' and connecting with our Spiritual Self we can finally tap into our awesome inner power to achieve the best in whatever we desire.

Would you like to: Live your life with faith and without fear? Find contentment and deep satisfaction? Tap into your passion, dreams and potential? Develop inner strength, confidence and self-belief? Free yourself to connect with your Spiritual Self? Be who you were born to be? If so this beautifully written book captures the essential qualities and fundamental principles for success in sport and life.

Combining her exceptional expertise in the field of peak performance coaching and personal & spiritual development, with inspirational verse, Helen K Emms coaches us to change disempowering mindsets and nurture our spirit.

CPSIA information can be obtained at www.ICGtesting.com
Printed in the USA
BVOW042210190212

283312BV00005B/1/P